The Modern Novel

Critical Approaches

Written and edited by Barbara Bleiman, Jane Ogborn and Lucy Webster

Design: Eamonn England
Additional design: Fran Stowell
Cover: Blaise Thompson
Editorial assistance: Lisa Hallgarten and Guido Martini
Printed by: Redwood Books
Published by The English & Media Centre, 18 Compton Terrace, London N1 2UN
© 2001
ISBN: 0 907016 71 5

Acknowledgements

Thanks to Pat Barker and Ian McEwan for their generous support of the project; Jenny Green for her helpful comments and suggestions on *Enduring Love*, and David Morgan for his essay on '*Regeneration* and the History of Psychoanalysis'.

Thanks also to: Pat Barker for extracts from *Regeneration* (Viking, 1991); Ian McEwan for extracts from *Enduring Love*, *The Cement Garden*, *The Child in Time*, *Black Dogs*, *Amsterdam* and *First Love Last Rites* (all published by Jonathan Cape); Carcanet Press Ltd for extracts from Robert Graves' *Goodbye to all That* (Penguin, rev.ed.1960); The Random House Group Ltd for an extract from *Slaughterhouse 5* by Kurt Vonnegut (Jonathan Cape); Sebastian Faulks for extracts from *Birdsong* (Hutchinson); John Keegan for extracts from *The First World War* (Hutchinson); Wilfred Owen's 'The Next War' from *The Poems of Wilfred Owen* (Chatto Poetry); Robert Wright for extracts from *The Moral Animal* (Little Brown & Co UK); Barbara Levy Literary Agency for the use of Siegfried Sassoon's poems 'Survivors' and 'Banishment' from *The War Poems* and 'Sassoon's Long Journey' from *The Complete Memoirs of George Sherston*; Faber and Faber Ltd for extracts from *Siegfried's Journey 1916-1920* by Siegfried Sassoon; Susan Hill for extracts from *Strange Meeting* (Penguin Books Ltd); Picador Classics for extracts from Erich Maria Remarque's *All Quiet on the Western Front*; Oxford University Press for extracts from Paul Fussell's *The Great War and Modern Memory*; Artificial Eye for extracts from their film version of Pat Barker's *Regeneration*; *World Socialist Web Site (*www.wsws.org) for their review of *Regeneration*; Samuel Hynes for an extract from his review of *Regeneration* published in *The New York Times* (March 29, 1992); *BBC Online*; *The Observer* for 'Whose Side are you On?' (© Melvyn Bragg 1999); *The Guardian* for several extracts and articles; *The Literary Review*; *The Village Voice*; *The Waterstone's Magazine*; *The New Statesman*; *The Independent/Syndication*; *The Financial Times*; *The New Republic*. Every effort has been made to trace and acknowledge copyright but if any accidental infringement has been made we would welcome information to redress the situation.

English & Media Centre

A personal reading

The questions listed here ask you to think about yourself as a reader of novels.
- Work through the questions on your own.

- What sort of reader are you? Fast? Slow? Persistent? Someone who gives up easily? How do you feel about reading a novel more than once?
- How many novels have you read in the last 6 -12 months? What, if anything, did they have in common? In your opinion, which was the best? Why?
- What would *you* list as the ingredients of a good novel?
- What puts you off a novel? What don't you like?
- What do you do about the parts you don't enjoy? What do you do about the parts you don't understand? Have you ever not finished a novel? What was it, and why did you stop reading? How far did you get before you gave up?
- How do you choose a novel? (Recommendations? Reviews in papers or magazines?)
- Do you ever talk to other people about what you read?
- Do you think there are 'men's novels' and 'women's novels'?
- What are you expecting from the novels you are going to read as set books for your AS/A Level exams?

- In small groups, take it in turns to share and reflect on your 'reading profiles'. What similarities and differences are there in your responses? What suggestions can you give each other for getting the most out of your reading on this course? Prepare to feed back your discoveries to the class.

Contents

Video contents	video timings

Enduring Love

Regeneration

Introduction

EMC Advanced Literature Series

EMC Advanced Literature Series is a resource for A Level English Literature (and elements of Language and Literature). It is designed to meet the requirements of the new AS/A2 specifications for 2000 in challenging, innovative and practical ways. Each publication includes:
- texts for study, both literary texts and extracts from literary criticism
- student activities
- teachers' notes.

Despite the shifts in emphasis implied by Assessment Objectives 4 and 5 – contextual issues and different interpretations – the text remains central. A Level students are still expected to focus primarily on the texts set for study in each module, and to:
- read closely and carefully
- get to know the text really well
- get below the surface and between the lines
- interpret and make meanings
- see patterns – big ones and small ones
- make links with other things they have read
- be alert to ways writers choose to use language.

The activities in all three sections of the book are intended to develop these critical reading skills. However, the resource is also intended to support teachers and students as they get to grips with the requirement to 'articulate independent opinions and judgements, informed by different interpretations of literary texts by other readers' (AO4); 'show understanding of the contexts in which literary texts are written and understood' (AO5i) and 'evaluate the significance of cultural, historical and other contextual influences upon literary texts and study' (AO5ii).

The Modern Novel – Critical Approaches

The book is divided into three sections:
- Approaches to the Modern Novel
- *Enduring Love* with a video interview with Ian McEwan
- *Regeneration* with a video interview with Pat Barker

There is also an edited CD- Rom version of the interviews, containing most of the key sections.

Section 1 – Approaches to the Modern Novel

Section 1 has been written for use with any of the modern novels studied at AS and A2. The first activities, exploring what is meant by 'modern' and 'novel' and the work on 'A personal reading profile', introduce students to AS level study in an accessible way. Students explore the narrative techniques and features of the novel through a series of practical activities; at each stage they are encouraged to experiment with the techniques in short pieces of creative writing and to apply what they have learned to their set text. Work on the development of the 'Literary Heritage' and the modern novel encourages students to think critically about the ways these labels are used and to see the novel they are studying within a continuing tradition.

Sections 2 and 3 – *Enduring Love* and *Regeneration*

The activities on both *Enduring Love* and *Regeneration* provide practical and engaging ways into key aspects of each novel, particularly those areas likely to prove most challenging to students at AS Level. It is not expected that teachers will use the book sequentially. However the teachers' notes do offer a possible route through each novel and the study material, with suggested strategies for the first reading. With *Enduring Love*, a planned approach to the first reading is particularly important, given that it has challenging elements for less experienced readers.

The video interviews could either be screened in stages during a first reading, or at one sitting soon after reading. It is worth bearing in mind, with *Enduring Love* in particular, that showing some sections of the video might give away plot and character information that could affect the first reading. We would, therefore, advise viewing the interview before showing it to your class.

The CD-Rom is intended as a useful addition to the video. It enables teachers to:
– find just one part of an interview more speedily than on video
– allow students access to the interview in pairs or small groups
– provide a Library copy, that students can access for themselves for independent study or revision.

The activities on both novels contain extensive contextual material and critical writing, to support AO4 and AO5. The contextual material on *Regeneration* includes extracts from letters, diaries, photos, autobiography, the film of Barker's novel, poems and extracts from other novels written about the war. This makes it particularly useful for students preparing for the synoptic paper for AQA A, whether they are studying *Regeneration* as a set text or not. The novel itself can be studied as one of the internal assessment texts for A2 in the AQA A specification. *Regeneration* also appears as a set text in the 2000 specifications for OCR and WJEC. *Enduring Love* is a set text for the 2000 specifications for AQA A and AQA B.

Quotations are taken from the following editions: *Enduring Love*, Vintage pbk, 1998 and *Regeneration*, Penguin pbk, 1982.

What is 'the modern novel'?

What is modern?

- Individually write your own definition of the word 'modern'. Illustrate your definition with examples of objects, people or ideas you would describe as modern. Use the ideas suggested here to start you thinking:
- contemporary
- happening now
- not old fashioned.

- Read your definitions to the class and come up with a list of everything this word means to you.

According to the *Oxford English Dictionary* 'modern English' is English from about 1500, and 'modern History' refers to history from the end of the Middle Ages.

- How do these uses of the word 'modern' compare with your ideas?

What is a novel?

- On your own, try to answer the question, 'What is a novel?' in as much detail as you can. Use the prompts suggested here to help you develop your definition.

- What are the essential ingredients of a novel?
- What makes a novel different from a short story, a memoir, an autobiography, a book about travel, a diary, a journal, a collection of letters or a news reports?
- What features does a novel share with these other forms of writing?

- Feed back your ideas and come up with as full a description of 'a novel' as you can.

Are they really 'novel'?

Today, the *Oxford English Dictionary* defines the word 'novel' as:
- a fictitious prose narrative of book length (from Italian – *novella storia* – 'new story)'
- interestingly new or unusual (from Latin *novellus*, from *novus* – 'new')

- Spend a few minutes talking about whether the novels you have read or studied meet either of these definitions. In what ways are they new?

The 'novel' as a literary form became established during the eighteenth and nineteenth centuries. A broad description which would cover most novels at this time is 'a long narrative, in prose, dealing mainly with contemporary people and society'. Its newness or 'novelty' came from the fact that it was in prose, and dealt with 'real' life.

Ian McEwan suggests that the original meaning of the word 'novel' is still very important:

> I think that what we're doing each time we sit down to a new novel, is new. I mean, that's right at the root of this word. We have to feel as a matter of working practice that we're doing something unlike anything else, otherwise there would be no reason to do it.

- How far does this description fit the novels you have read? Is there anything about it which you want to challenge?

Statements about the novel

Printed below and on page 9 are some statements about what 'the novel' is, by both pre-twentieth and twentieth century writers.

- Read through the statements on your own, highlighting or underlining anything which strikes you as interesting or surprising.

- Choose one or two statements which match your own definition of the novel. Are there any statements you disagree with or want to challenge? Do any of the statements cause you to re-think your definition of the novel? If so, in what ways?

- In pairs or small groups, share your responses to the statements.

- As a class, talk about the ways in which the idea of the novel has changed since it was first defined as a literary form, over two hundred years ago. Has anything remained the same throughout this time? Who challenges or contradicts previously accepted ideas? When, and in what ways?

1   The Novel is a picture of real life and manners, and of the times in which it is written ... The Novel gives a familiar relation of such things, as pass every day before our eyes, such as may happen to our friend, or to ourselves; and the perfection of it is, to represent in every scene, in so easy and natural a manner, and to make them appear so probable, as to deceive us into a persuasion (at least while we are reading) that all is real, until we are affected by the joys or distresses, of the persons in the story, as if they were our own.

The Progress of Romance, **Clara Reeve, 1785**

2   a smooth tale, generally of love

Dr Johnson, 1709-84

3   We find here a close imitation of man and manners; we see the very web and texture of society as it really exists, and as we meet it when we come into the world. If poetry has something 'more divine' in it, this savours more of humanity. We are brought acquainted with the motives and characters of mankind, imbibe our notions of virtue and vice from practical examples, and are taught a knowledge of the world through the airy medium of romance.

William Hazlitt, 1778-1830

4   No novel is anything, for the purposes either of comedy or tragedy, unless the reader can sympathise with the characters whose names he finds upon the page.

Autobiography, **Anthony Trollope, 1883**

5   The novel is a formidable mass, and it is so amorphous ... It is most distinctly one of the moister areas of literature – irrigated by a hundred rills and occasionally degenerating into swamp.

Aspects of the Novel, **E.M.Forster, 1927**

6   The novelist, whoever he is and whenever he is writing, is giving form to a story, giving form to his moral and metaphysical views, and giving form to his particular experiences of sensations, people, places and society.

The Appropriate Form: An essay on the novel, **Barbara Hardy, 1964**

7   *Faulkner:* A writer needs three things, experience, observation and imagination, any two of which, at times any one of which, can supply the lack of the others. With me a story usually begins with a single idea or memory or mental picture. The writing of the story is simply a matter of working up to that moment, to explain why it happened or what it caused to follow. A writer is trying to create believable people in credible, moving situations in the most moving way he can. Obviously he must use as one of his tools the environment which he knows ...
Interviewer: Some people say they can't understand your writing, even after they read it two or three times. What approach would you suggest for them?
Faulkner: Read it four times.

From an interview with Jean Stein (1956), quoted in *Writers at Work*, Ed. Kay Dick, 1972

8   Anything that wants to call itself a novel is a novel, by definition, so fiction can do anything it wants to do. I think it can do more things than we tend to think it can. The novel has some role and responsibility in helping to explain experience and making the world comprehensible, even if it's only to the person who is writing it.

Angela Carter in interview with John Haffenden
***Novelists in Interview*, 1985**

9   I still 'believe' that it is worthwhile creating that effect of recognition which the classic realist text can produce, that sense of fidelity to history and to social texture. I like to give that to my readers, but I don't any longer think that it is enough to do just that ... like all modern novelists from Henry James onwards, I write layered fiction, so that it will make sense and give satisfaction even on the surface level, while there are other levels of implication and references that are there to be discovered by those who have the interest or motivation to do so.

David Lodge in interview with John Haffenden
***Novelists in Interview*, 1985**

10   The novel has from its very beginnings had an equivocal status, somewhere between a work of art and a commodity; but in the twentieth century, under the impact of modernism, it seemed to split into two kinds of fiction – the highbrow novel of aesthetic ambition, which sold in small numbers to a discriminating elite, and the popular or middlebrow novel of entertainment which sold in much larger numbers to a mass audience. Now the gap seems to be narrowing again.

The Practice of Writing, **David Lodge, 1996**

11   I think the novel as a form is a marvellous means of investigation into life, and I mean life in all its senses, daily life, ordinary life, emotional life, life as we try to give meaning to it and try to understand it. I think it does it better than any other form, largely because it can give the illusion of getting inside the minds of other people. And I think having a theory of other people's minds, having a sense of what it's like to be someone else, is one of the great gifts we have. It makes us capable of living with each other, because we have some sense of empathy, or what it might be like to be someone completely different from ourselves.

Ian McEwan in an English & Media Centre interview, 2000

The history of the novel

Exploring the 'Literary Heritage Novel'

The 'Literary Heritage' timeline on pages 12–15 is a 'sketch map' of the development of the English novel, from its beginnings in the eighteenth century to the early part of the twentieth century. It is an attempt to show where novels written today have come from, or what they are written in reaction against.

The timeline focuses on the 'canon' of English novelists, as reflected in the list of pre-1914 authors named in the National Curriculum. In a very simplified form, it provides an overview of the following:
– how 'the novel' began
– how it grew and developed during the eighteenth and nineteenth centuries
– the point at which writers began to experiment with the 'novel' as a literary form
– the ways in which writers build on and react against the kinds of novels written by their predecessors.

● Read the timeline, highlighting or annotating it with anything which interests you.

This 'Literary Heritage' timeline is only a partial account of the history of the novel. It:
– does not show many of the genres you may enjoy reading, such as historical romances, science fiction, magical realism and so on
– doesn't include many of the novels which were written by women, such as Mrs Radcliffe and Maria Edgeworth
– does not include 'popular' novels
– does not include the nineteenth century European and Russian writers such as Balzac, Zola and Proust in France, and Dostoyevsky, Turgenev and Tolstoy in Russia, who greatly influenced English authors.

● Talk about why you think these writers and novels have been omitted from the 'canon'.

A modern novel?

● Read the timeline again, this time stopping after each stage to talk about the ways in which the later novels are similar to, and different from, the earlier ones.

Not a line but a map

Because this timeline (and indeed any timeline) can only represent one version of the rise of the novel, it gives the impression that the novels themselves are limited. This, of course, is not the case. The novel has always been a very flexible kind of writing, as the quotations below suggest.

> fiction can do anything it wants to do
> **Angela Carter in interview with John Haffenden, 1985**

> The astonishing variety of styles on offer today, as if in an aesthetic supermarket, includes traditional as well as innovative styles, minimalism as well as excess, nostalgia as well as prophecy ... what we have now is a literary situation in which everything is in and nothing is out.
> **'The Novelist Today' in** *The Practice of Writing,* **David Lodge, 1996**

In the nineteenth century the growth of the novel's popularity was explosive. In the twentieth century the variety of novels being written has been similarly explosive. The world map on page 16 shows some of the key novelists writing in English in the later part of the twentieth century.

- Spend a few minutes studying the map and talking about what you notice.

- Take responsibility for one of the writers listed on the map of the world and find an extract of their work. Annotate this extract to show what you find interesting or striking about it. As a class, share your discoveries about the extracts.

- Talk about other ways these writers could be grouped together, for instance writers from the world map could be combined with those from the 'Literary Heritage' timeline by bringing together all the novels written in the same genre.

Grouping by genre

The last 50 years or so have also seen a huge increase in the number of writers playing with genres, combining them in different and surprising ways, for example romance and science fiction.

- As a class, think of the ways in which you could group the novels you have read by genre, for example as science fiction, autobiography, biography, thriller or gothic horror. Do any novels belong to more than one genre?

A literary dinner party

The novelist and critic, E. M. Forster had a go at grouping together writers from different periods. Instead of listing the writers chronologically, he described all the English writers as 'seated together in a circular room all writing their novels simultaneously'. This let him pair up writers who he thought wrote in similar ways even though they lived in different historical periods. For instance, Lawrence Sterne might sit near Virginia Woolf who was writing 150 years later as both were interested in capturing the complexity of an individual's thoughts.

- Imagine you are throwing a dinner party for a group of writers from any period of history and country. Who would you invite? Who would you sit together at dinner? Who else do you think they would enjoy mingling with? Are there any writers who you think should be kept well apart? Are there any writers who have so little in common they would have nothing to say to each other?

- Take it turns to read out your guest lists and the reasons for your decisions.

The 'Literary Heritage' time line

The novel in the C18: beginnings

Daniel Defoe
1660-1731

The Life and Strange Surprising Adventures of Robinson Crusoe (1719)

Uses real life incidents, factual information and episodic narratives to create illusion of reality.

Fortunes & Misfortunes of the Famous Moll Flanders (1722)

Journal of the Plague Year (1722)

Samuel Richardson
1689-1761

Pamela or Virtue Rewarded (1740-41)

Clarissa (1747-48)

Novels written in letters between characters. In both novels the chaste heroine resists seduction – Pamela marries well; Clarissa dies. Serious moral purpose + psychological insight.

Henry Fielding
1707-1754

Joseph Andrews (1742)

A parody of *Pamela*. Comic use of the stubbornly virtuous hero in a series of awkward situations.

Tom Jones (1749)

Comic epic: characters are a wide range of social types, not explored as individuals. Fielding interrupts his narratives with personal comments and opinions about human experience.

Lawrence Sterne
1713-1768

The Life and Opinions of Tristram Shandy (1760-67)

Pretends to be an autobiographical novel, but full of flashbacks, digressions and tricks of layout. Intended to challenge readers' expectations of straightforward 'biographical' narratives like most of those listed so far.

The novel in the C19: developments

Sir Walter Scott
1771-1832

12 novels including:
Waverley (1814)

First of a series of 8 historical novels set in C17 & C18 Scotland.

Ivanhoe (1819)

Another historical novel, set in C11 England. Scott was the first novelist to emphasise the relationship between characters and the society or environment of which they are a part.

Jane Austen
1775-1817

Sense & Sensibility (1811)
Pride & Prejudice (1813)
Mansfield Park (1814)
Emma (1816)
Northanger Abbey (pub. 1818)
Persuasion (pub. 1818)

Her novels focus on middle and upper class provincial society, in realistic contemporary settings. When presenting characters she combines perceptive, witty observation and psychological insight. *Northanger Abbey* and *Persuasion* (her first and last) were published after her death. Austen was not a 'best seller' during her life time – she had to finance the publication of *Sense & Sensibility* herself, but is now considered one of the greatest English novelists.

Mary Shelley
1797-1851

*Frankenstein
or the Modern Prometheus* (1818)

Inspired by a dream, and written as part of a competition with her husband, the poet Shelley, and Lord Byron, Shelley combines many different genres in this novel – the gothic or novel of terror, aspects of science fiction, the novel of ideas and psychology. In addition she uses a variety of forms – letters, diary entries, memoir, and multiple narrators.

The novel in the C19: growth

During the C19 there was a huge explosion of fiction in England, due partly to an increase in readers especially from the middle classes, and partly to methods of publication and availability of novels to readers. In 1821 Scott's publisher was the first to market his novels in the 3 volume format – a big advantage to libraries and to readers who could not afford to buy the books for themselves. At the same time, magazines were beginning to publish novels as serials, in weekly or monthly parts. Both these methods of publication influenced the form and structure of the novel, as well as its content, availability and popularity.

William Makepeace Thackeray
1811-1863

6 major novels including:
Vanity Fair (1848)

Social satire of the English upper middle classes.

Charles Dickens
1812-1870

17 novels including:
Oliver Twist (1837-8)
Christmas Carol (1843)
David Copperfield (1849-50)
Bleak House (1852-3)
Hard Times (1854)
Great Expectations (1860-61)

Hugely popular writer, combining comedy, sentimentality, melodrama, social comment and criticism.

Anthony Trollope
1815-1882

6 'Barsetshire' novels including:
The Warden (1855)
Last Chronicle of Barset (1867)

Carefully developed characters, set in a fictional cathedral city.

6 more novels including:
The Way We Live Now (1875)
The Prime Minister (1876)

Mainly set in London, with background of contemporary politics.

Wilkie Collins
1824-1889

The Woman in White (1860)
The Moonstone   (1868)

One of the originators of the detective story. Friend of, and collaborator with Dickens.

The C19 also saw an increase in the number of novels written by women

Charlotte Bronte
1816-1855

4 novels including:
Jane Eyre   (1847)
Villette   (1853)

First person narratives. Published under a male pseudonym, exploring the emotional lives of her heroines.

Emily Bronte
1818-1848

Wuthering Heights   (1847)

First person narrative. Many people scandalised by its style, particularly the use of dialect and content – even when they thought it was written by a man. Innovative structure.

Anne Bronte
1820-1849

Agnes Grey   (1847)
The Tenant of Wildfell Hall   (1848)

Not a named pre-1900 author in the National Curriculum... but nor are Aphra Behn (1640-1689), Fanny Burney (1752-1840), Maria Edgeworth (1767-1869) or many other women writers popular in their day.

Mrs Gaskell
1810-1865

6 novels including:
Mary Barton   (1848)
North & South (1854-5)

'Social problem' novels, set in Manchester, dealing with issues of poverty and class.

George Eliot (Mary Ann Evans)
1819-1880

7 novels including:
The Mill on the Floss (1860)
Silas Marner   (1861)
Middlemarch   (1871-2)

Novels mainly set in the Midlands countryside. Concerned with the individual in relation to the society within which they live.

Four novelists who make a bridge between the earlier C19 novel, and the 'modern' novel of the C20

Thomas Hardy
1840-1928

14 novels including:
The Mayor of Casterbridge   (1886)
Tess of the d'Urbervilles   (1891)
Jude the Obscure   (1895)

Novels of character and environment. Novels are set in Wessex – Hardy's re-creation of the south west of England – and deal with the effects of fate and society on the individual.

Joseph Conrad
1857-1924

17 novels including:
Heart of Darkness (1902)

A Polish seaman, widely travelled; deals with issues of identity, isolation and political power. Also technically innovative, experimenting with different narrators and ways of handling narrative sequence.

Henry James
1843-1916

15 novels including:
Washington Square (1880)
Portrait of a Lady (1881)

American, but settled in England. Naturalised British in 1915. Novels reflect his interest in the clash between American and European cultures, and his ideas about 'the novel' as art, rather than a purely realistic version of life.

Robert Louis Stevenson
1850-1894

5 novels including:
Treasure Island (1883)
The Strange Case of Dr Jekyll & Mr Hyde (1886)

Stevenson's novels are adventure stories, historical romances and psychological explorations – a wider range of genres than his predecessors.

The novel in the C20: beginnings of the 'modern 'novel

What makes these 'Modern' is their developments and experiments with how to write fiction, the different ways they use language, and subject matter and ideas which had not been explored in this way before.

James Joyce
1882-1941
Dubliners (1914)

Collection of short stories, unified by the Dublin setting, use of Irish speech rhythms, and blend of realism and symbolism.

Portrait of the Artist as a Young Man (1916)

Autobiographical novel with innovative uses of language to parallel the hero's growth from child to man.

Ulysses (1922)

Novel traces a single day in the lives of three Dublin characters. Inventive uses of language, handling of time and overall structure of the text, which is based on Homer's *Odyssey*.

D.H. Lawrence
1885-1930

10 novels including:
Sons & Lovers (1913)

The Rainbow (1915)
Women in Love (1921)

Autobiographical novel set in Nottinghamshire; 3rd person narrator. Also set in the Midlands; both novels explore relationships between men and women, including aspects of sexuality. *The Rainbow*, like *Lady Chatterley's Lover*, was initially banned for immorality.

Virginia Woolf
1882-1941
9 novels including:
Mrs Dalloway (1925)

In reaction against the usual emphasis on plot and story, she experimented with the 'stream of consciousness' technique, to convey her characters' inner experience.

To the Lighthouse (1927)

Novelists writing in English

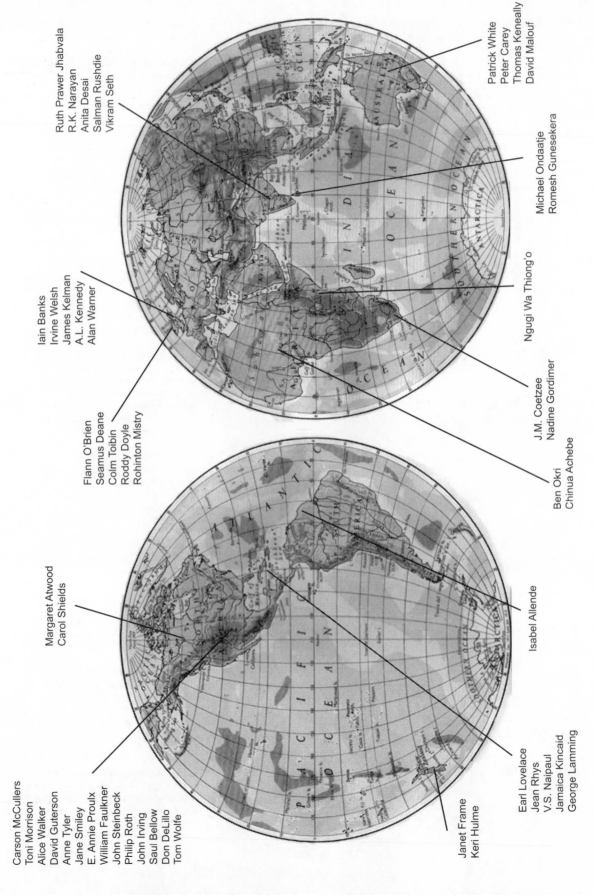

Ruth Prawer Jhabvala
R.K. Narayan
Anita Desai
Salman Rushdie
Vikram Seth

Patrick White
Peter Carey
Thomas Keneally
David Malouf

Michael Ondaatje
Romesh Gunesekera

Iain Banks
Irvine Welsh
James Kelman
A.L. Kennedy
Alan Warner

Ngugi Wa Thiong'o

Flann O'Brien
Seamus Deane
Colm Toibin
Roddy Doyle
Rohinton Mistry

J.M. Coetzee
Nadine Gordimer

Ben Okri
Chinua Achebe

Margaret Atwood
Carol Shields

Isabel Allende

Carson McCullers
Toni Morrison
Alice Walker
David Guterson
Anne Tyler
Jane Smiley
E. Annie Proulx
William Faulkner
John Steinbeck
Philip Roth
John Irving
Saul Bellow
Don DeLillo
Tom Wolfe

Janet Frame
Keri Hulme

Earl Lovelace
Jean Rhys
V.S. Naipaul
Jamaica Kincaid
George Lamming

What makes a novel 'modern'?

Features of the modern novel

Listed below are some of the features often associated with those novels described as 'modern'.

- Read through the list and talk about any novels you have read which included these features. Could you apply these features to films, or music, or art?

- Add any other features which you think are important to the modern novel.

A wide range of different genres is available to the novelist.

The writer may use a mixture of genres within one text.

The text draws attention to the fact that it is constructed.

The sequence of the narrative is often disrupted by flashbacks and flash-forwards, gaps and repetition.

The inner lives and motivation of characters are at least as, or even more important than, external events.

The writer introduces a variety of different kinds of writing into the text, for example letters and documents.

The writer is concerned with philosophical, scientific or other issues and ideas important in the contemporary world.

The modern novel expects the reader to work hard and contribute to the meaning, for example filling in the gaps and keeping track of who is narrating the story.

- Look again at the 'Literary Heritage' timeline on pages 12-15 and the list of statements about the novel on pages 8-9. How many of the defining features suggested here can you find in the 'Literary Heritage' timeline? Talk about anything which interests or surprises you. What features does the book you are studying share with these novels? What about the novels you read for pleasure?

Narrative and the novel

Representing reality

Novels are constructs, existing only in the imagination of the writer and reader. They are not real life. Some writers aim to create a convincing reflection of real life. Other writers draw attention to the fact that the world of the novel is *not* the real world. In this section, you will have the chance to explore some of the choices the writer makes when creating the fictional world of the novel.

Essential ingredients

All novelists work with the same four basic ingredients: story, plot, characters and setting.

How the novelist uses these ingredients is much more varied. In deciding how to tell their story, each novelist is faced with choices to make and problems to solve. These include:
– who tells the story and how
– how the story is organised
– how the characters are presented
– how the 'world' which they inhabit is made convincing and 'real' to the reader.

● Add any other things which you think the novelist has to decide when telling a story.

Story and plot – what's the difference?

● Read E.M. Forster's definition of the difference between a 'story' and a 'plot'.

> Let us define a plot. We have defined a story as a narrative of events arranged in their time sequence. A plot is also a narrative of events, the emphasis falling on causality. 'The king died and then the queen died,' is a story. 'The king died and then the queen died of grief,' is a plot. The time sequence is preserved, but the sense of causality overshadows it. Or again: 'The queen died, no one knew why, until it was discovered that it was through grief at the death of the king.' This is a plot with a mystery in it, a form capable of high development. It suspends the time sequence, it moves as far away from the story as its limitations will allow. Consider the death of the queen. If it is in a story we say 'and then?' If it is in a plot we ask 'why?'
>
> *Aspects of the Novel*, **E.M.Forster**

Printed below are the stories of *Pride and Prejudice* and *Of Mice and Men*.

> Elizabeth Bennett meets Mr Darcy, and dislikes him. He proposes, she rejects him, but gradually realises she was wrong about him. She accepts his second proposal and they marry.
>
> George and Lenny arrive together at the ranch. Lennie kills Curley's wife and George shoots him. George is left alone.

● Annotate these 'stories' with the questions you need answering to turn the story into a plot, for example, 'Why does Elizabeth dislike Mr Darcy?'

The story of your novel

● In pairs, have a go at turning the novel you are studying into a three sentence 'story'. Remember, you are only answering the question, 'What happens next?'

● Take it in turns to read out your stories and come up with a version which you can all accept.

● Talk about all the different things which the 'story' lacks in comparison with the novel. What choices does the novelist have to make when planning how to turn a story into a plot?

Beginnings, middles and ends

Telling stories

The extract printed here is from the novel *Slaughterhouse 5* by Kurt Vonnegut. In it the first person narrator explains the way in which he has told his story.

● Read the extract and talk about the ideas it raises about telling stories.

> As a trafficker in climaxes and thrills and characterization and wonderful dialogue and suspense and confrontations, I had outlined the Dresden story many times. The best outline I ever made, or anyway the prettiest one, was on the back of a roll of wallpaper.
>
> I used my daughter's crayons, a different color for each main character. One end of the wallpaper was the beginning of the story, and the other end was the end, and then there was all that middle part, which was the middle. And the blue line met the red line and then the yellow line, and the yellow line stopped because the character represented by the yellow line was dead. And so on. The destruction of Dresden was represented by a vertical band of orange cross-hatching, and all the lines that were still alive passed through it, came out the other side.

Exploring beginnings

In the following article Blake Morrison suggests that opening sentences of novels can be organised into different categories.

● Read through the article and try to decide which category most accurately fits the novel you are studying.

● Try to apply these categories to other novels you have read or studied.

How to hook them from the start
Blake Morrison examines the art of the intro.
Beginnings matter. They always have. Middles have no limits – they can scrunch up or they can sprawl. Endings may be left open, ambiguous, incomplete. But no novel has ever not begun. And if it doesn't begin right, the suspicion is that the rest of it won't be right either. Gabriel García Márquez has said that he sometimes spends months on a first paragraph, since it's there that the theme, style and tone of a book are defined – solve that and the rest comes easily.

In an age of multiple choice and short attention spans, beginnings are more crucial than ever. To prevent readers drifting off, an author has to hook them quickly. As the novelist

Brian Moore once put it, once you've read 20 or 30 pages by a writer, and want to continue, 'you are in his sea and swimming in that sea': he can write quite badly and you'll stick with him.

…

A survey of past and present practice does suggest certain common strategies for beginning a novel:

The Plunge: Horace in *Ars Poetica* talks of the desirability of hurrying readers into the middle of things – *in medias res* – as though they knew the story already. Graham Greene does this in *Brighton Rock*: 'Hale knew they meant to murder him before he had been in Brighton three hours.' Other novelists begin mid-conversation, like Dickens with Gradgrind in *Hard Times*: 'Now what I want is, Facts.' David Storey kicks off *This Sporting Life*, mid-scrum:

'I had my head to Mellor's backside, waiting for the ball to come between his legs.'

The Shocker: Kafka's *Metamorphosis* is the prime example: 'As Gregor Samsa awoke one morning from uneasy dreams he found himself transformed in his bed into a gigantic insect.' Will Self pays homage to Kafka in the second of the two novellas that comprise his terrific *Cock and Bull*: 'Bull, a large and heavyset young man, awoke one morning to find that while he had slept he had acquired another primary sexual characteristic: to whit, a vagina.'

The Intriguing Narrator: 'If I am out of my mind, it's all right with me,' begins Saul Bellow's *Herzog*, immediately engaging us with the hero, who, if that's his attitude, we feel we're going to like. Günter Grass does something similar, if more extreme, in *The Tin Drum*: 'Granted: I am an inmate of a mental hospital; my keeper is watching me, he never lets me out of his sight ...' F. Scott Fitzgerald takes the opposite tack in *The Great Gatsby*, of course, allowing the colourless Nick Carraway to lead us through events.

The Epigram: [The epigram is exemplified by Austen and Tolstoy] 'It is a truth universally acknowledged, that a single man in possession of a good fortune, must be in want of a wife.' (*Pride and Prejudice* by Jane Austen) 'All happy families resemble one another, but each unhappy family is unhappy in its own way.' (*Anna Karenina* by Leo Tolstoy)

The Promise: 'This is the saddest story I have ever heard,' begins Ford Maddox Ford's *The Good Soldier*, inviting us to be moved too. The promise that the events about to be recounted truly took place – the avowal of authenticity – has been a common device since the 18th century. A recent example is Kurt Vonnegut's *Slaughterhouse-Five*: 'All this happened, more or less.'

The Omen: If you are going to make a book end badly, said Robert Louis Stevenson, it must end badly from the beginning. John Updike, in *Rabbit at Rest*, actually uses the word 'ominous' in an opener that hints very heavily how the book will conclude: 'Standing amid the tan, excited post-Christmas crowd at the Southwest Florida Regional Airport, Rabbit Angstrom has a funny sudden feeling that what he has come to meet, what's floating in unseen about to land, is not his son Nelson and daughter-in-law Pru and their two children but something more ominous and intimately his: his own death.'

The Particulars: Some novelists write as if they were reporters on the old *Sunday Times* Insight team, bedding their story down in straws of meticulous detail. Bruce Chatwin begins his novel *Utz* thus: 'An hour before dawn on March 7th 1974, Kaspar Joachim Utz died of a second and long expected stroke, in his apartment at no 5 Siroka Street, overlooking the Old Jewish Cemetery in Prague.' Many 19th century novels do the same.

The Self-referral: Some narrators feel self-conscious about the act of storytelling. Rider Haggard's *King Solomon's Mines*: 'It is a curious thing that at my age – 55 last birthday – I should find myself taking up a pen ...' Holden Caulfield in Salinger's *Catcher in the Rye* is awkward too: 'If you really want to hear about it, the first thing you'll probably want to know is where I was born, and what my lousy childhood was like ...' The most self-conscious beginning ever is perhaps Italo Calvino's *If on a winter's night a traveller*: 'You are about to begin reading Italo Calvino's new novel *If on a winter's night a traveller*.'

There it is: plenty of strategies to choose from. To the narrator of Graham Greene's *The End of the Affair* it can't help but be a random business: 'arbitrarily one chooses that moment of experience from which to look back or from which to look ahead.' Perhaps all that counts is that readers feel confident that the author knows what he or she is doing, and has taken pains to get it right ...

Blake Morrison, *The Independent on Sunday*, September 26th 1999

Exploring endings

Deciding how to end the novel is one of the biggest problems a writer has to solve. In the nineteenth century the novelist often used the final chapter to tie up the loose ends, sort the characters out and usually marry them off. In terms of plot, marriage is seen as the end (or the purpose) for women, as well as The End of the story the novelist has been telling. In the twentieth century novels this convention has been turned on its head – the neat ending is more often abandoned in favour of a much more uncertain and often ambiguous conclusion.

The *Oxford English Dictionary* defines 'End' as:
- the final part of something
- the furthest or most extreme part
- a termination of a state or situation
- a person's death or downfall
- a goal or desired result
- a small piece that is left after use.

● Talk about the different ideas raised by these definitions. What insights do they give you into the ways in which a novel might end?

● Printed below are the endings of nine novels from the nineteenth and twentieth centuries. How do the dictionary definitions of 'end' apply to these literary endings?

● On pages 19 and 20, Blake Morrison defines eight different ways in which a novel can begin. On your own come up with eight different categories of endings for a novel. Some suggestions are given here:
  - abrupt
  - weird
  - narrator's voice.

● Try and fit the endings printed here into your categories.

● Take it in turns to read out your categories and the endings you have placed in each category. You should be prepared to explain both the criteria you used when coming up with the categories and the reasons you had for putting each ending into a particular category.

1 I took her hand in mine, and we went out of the ruined place; and, as the morning mists had risen long ago when I first left the forge, so the evening mists were rising now, and in all the broad expanse of tranquil light they showed to me, I saw no shadow of another parting from her.

Great Expectations, **Charles Dickens, 1860-61**

2 Tom's most well, now, and got his bullet around his neck on a watch guard for a watch, and is always seeing what time it is, and so there ain't nothing more to write about, and I am rotten glad of it, because if I'd a knowed what a trouble it was to make a book I wouldn't a tackled it and ain't agoing to no more. But I reckon I got to light out for the Territory ahead of the rest, because Aunt Sally she's going to adopt me and sivilise me and I can't stand it. I been there before.
THE END. YOURS TRULY, HUCK FINN.

Huckleberry Finn, **Mark Twain, 1885**

3 The tomb bore the names of Tom and Maggie Tulliver, and below their names it was written: 'In their death they were not divided.'

The Mill on the Floss, **George Eliot, 1860**

4 Now you are man and wife, Reader and Reader. A great double bed receives your parallel readings.

Ludmilla closes her book, turns off her light, puts her head back against the pillow, and says, 'Turn off your light, too. Aren't you tired of reading?'

And you say, 'Just a moment, I've almost finished *If on a winter's night a traveller* by Italo Calvino (1979).'

If on a winter's night a traveller, **Italo Calvino, 1979**

5 I was damn near bawling, I felt so damn happy, if you want to know the truth. I don't know why. It was just that she looked so damn *nice*, the way she kept going round and round, in her blue coat and all. God, I wish you could've been there.

The Catcher in the Rye, **J.D. Salinger, 1951**

6 Are there any questions?

The Handmaid's Tale, **Margaret Atwood, 1985**

7 But you, O my brothers, remember sometimes thy little Alex that was. Amen. And all that cal.

A Clockwork Orange, **Anthony Burgess, 1962**

8 Every day brought him some new material. The story of this man who had killed a messenger and hanged himself would make interesting reading. One could almost write a whole chapter on him. Perhaps not a whole chapter but a reasonable paragraph, at any rate. There was so much else to include, and one must be firm in cutting out details. He had already chosen the title of the book, after much thought:*The Pacification of the Primitive Tribes of the Lower Niger*.

Things Fall Apart, **Chinua Achebe, 1958**

9 By and by all trace is gone, and what is forgotten is not only the footprints but the water too and what is down there. The rest is weather. Not the breath of the disremembered and unaccounted for, but wind in the eaves, or spring ice thawing too quickly. Just weather. Certainly no clamor for a kiss.

Beloved.

Beloved, **Toni Morrison, 1987**

From beginning to end – logging the changes

- Use a chart like the one shown here to help you record what happens between the opening sentence of the novel you are studying and the end, in no more than five stages. Don't worry yet about filling in the final two columns, 'Why?' and 'How?'.

What happens next?	Why?	How?

Writing your own story – 'The Murder'

Printed below is the beginning of a story called 'The Murder'.

> A woman murdered her husband.

The story ends with the sentence:

> The woman is now a famous doctor.

- In no more than five sentences, write a skeleton middle for this story, highlighting the changes which transform the initial situation (beginning) into the resolution (end). Focus on *what* happens, not *why* it happens.

Middles

Logging the changes which take place in the 'story' highlights the importance of the middle section of the novel. The middle shows *how* these changes are brought about.

- Return to your chart on the novel you are studying. Fill in the second and third columns, exploring the *reasons* for the changes and how the writer brings these about. Compare your analysis with those of other people in the class.

- Use what you have discovered about your novel to help you develop your own story into a plot. Annotate your skeleton outline of 'The Murder' to suggest possible reasons for the changes which take it from the beginning to the end.

What is really essential to the plot?

Novelists tell their stories through a series of episodes. Some of these short scenes are essential to developing the plot and moving the action on. Others are subsidiary. These supplement the essential episodes or add to the mood and atmosphere, but they do not move the action on.

For these activities you should use the novel you are studying for your AS or A2 course.

- Choose one episode which you think is essential to the plot and one which you think is subsidiary. What does the subsidiary one contribute to the novel in other ways? Take it in turns to introduce and justify your choices to the rest of the class.

- Work in pairs and take it in turns to open the novel at random. Skim read the episode you have opened it at and decide whether it is essential or subsidiary. Are you in agreement? Are there any sections where it is difficult to tell whether or not it is essential to the plot?

- Is it possible to have more than one essential plot? Can a sub-plot be essential or is it always subsidiary? Focus your discussion on both the novel you are studying now and any others that several of you have read in the past.

Beginning, middle and end – breaking the rules

Is a novel really as simple as beginning + middle + end? Do all novels fit this pattern?

- Talk about how well the beginning, middle and end structure describes the novel you are studying. Does the writer use, ignore, subvert or adapt it? If so, how does he or she do this and to what effect?

How is the story organised?

Handling time – exploring the novel you are studying

The last activity shows that although a novel has to begin and end somewhere, a writer is free to choose the order in which he or she places the events. The two different 'times' can be distinguished as:
— chronological time (the order in which the events in the novel took place)
— narrative time (the order in which the story is told and in which the reader encounters each event).

Sometimes chronological time and narrative time coincide, but they do not have to, for example the opening page of the novel might be the end of the story, with the rest told in flashback.

● As a class, make a list of all the different ways in which a writer can use and manipulate time in the novel. Use the suggestions given here to get you started:
— set the whole story in the past
— weave together a story told in the past with one set in the present.

Exploring time in your novel

How has the author of the novel you are studying handled time?

● Make a chart such as the one below, showing some of the main events of the novel as they occur in narrative time. Then re-arrange them in chronological order.

Narrative time	Chronological time

● Highlight any points where the writer has to deal with a jump in time. Look back at the novel and examine how they do this, for example by using a trigger phrase such as 'next day' or '3 years later', with a summary, or by changing the narrator.

● As a class, share your discoveries about the structure of the novel and narrative time.

'The Murder'

● Consolidate your understanding of the ways in which time can be handled in a novel by experimenting with the narrative time of your story, 'The Murder'. Choose where to start it and where to end it, not necessarily following chronological time.

Narrative voice

Who tells the story, and how?

One important decision a writer has to make is whether to tell the story in the first or third person.

First person narratives

First person narratives are told from the point of view of a character in the story.

A first person narrator:
- tells the story using 'I'
- can be the central figure in the story
- can be a character within the story, with a background and personality of his or her own but telling the story of the other characters
- cannot enter the consciousness of other characters or tell the story from their points of view
- establishes a sense of intimacy with the reader
- gives the reader direct insight into his or her thoughts and feelings
- may be unreliable or untrustworthy.

Narrators may be 'unreliable' because the writer has decided:
- to limit their knowledge or understanding of the events and people they describe
- to make them biased about the people and events they describe
- to give them questionable moral values
- to make the reader work harder at piecing together the 'truth' in the novel.

Third person narratives

Third person narratives can be told from an external point of view. This sort of narrative can give the reader the impression that no-one other than the writer is telling the story. Third person narratives can also be told from the point of view of one of the characters in the story.

A third person narrator:
- need not be a character in the story
- can be omniscient, all knowing, about events and people
- can seem distant, leaving the reader to interpret the events and behaviour of the cast of characters
- can intervene with comments and opinions on the action
- can enter into the consciousness of one or more of the characters, reflecting his or her thoughts and feelings and telling the story from that point of view
- can move between a point of view outside the characters and a point of view which is located close to, or inside the head of one of the characters.

A writer who chooses to tell the story in the third person can reveal the thoughts and feelings of the characters in several different ways:
- direct speech: the exact words of the character are quoted
- reported speech
- free indirect speech.
In free indirect speech, tags like 'he said' or 'she thought' are left out. The reader is brought into the head of the character, able to experience thoughts and feelings without the intervention of the narrator. When this is done well, the narrative picks up the tone and kind of language that a character would naturally use.

Interior monologues or stream of consciousness writing

At the beginning of the twentieth century some writers, for example James Joyce and Virginia Woolf, experimented with extending free indirect speech into 'stream of consciousness' writing. In this sort of writing the reader is taken right into the head of the character from whose point of view the story is being told. Unlike in a first person narrative, the character is still referred to as 'he' or 'she' or by their name.

Included here are some short quotations from the novel, *Regeneration*. Pat Barker's novel illustrates the different possibilities open to the writer when deciding how to tell a third person narrative.

- In pairs, read the extracts carefully and decide which technique they demonstrate.

- As a class, talk about the different effects each technique achieves.

1   Prior had lost weight during his time in sick bay. Watching the light fall on to his face, Rivers noticed how sharp his cheekbones had become.

2   Rivers let him continue. This had been Prior's attitude throughout the three weeks they'd spent trying to recover his memories of France. He seemed to be saying, 'All right. You can make me dredge up horrors, you can make me remember the deaths, but you will never make me feel.'

3   Sassoon leant out of the carriage window, still half-expecting to see Graves come pounding along the platform, looking even more dishevelled than usual.

4   Rivers waited.
'I mean, there was the riding, hunting, cricketing me, and then there was the ... the other side ... that was interested in poetry and music, and things like that. And I didn't seem able to ...' He laced his fingers. 'Knot them together.'
'And the third?'
'I'm sorry?'
'You said three.'
'Did I? I meant two.'
Ah. 'And then the war. You joined up on the first day.'

Choosing a narrative voice

The chart on page 27 summarises, in a simplified form, the choices each writer is faced with when deciding from whose point of view to tell the story.

- Look closely at the novel you are studying and talk about the different types of narration used. Pay particular attention to any points where there is a shift in the technique used, or in the point of view from which the story is told. Use the chart on page 27 and the descriptions on page 25 to help you.

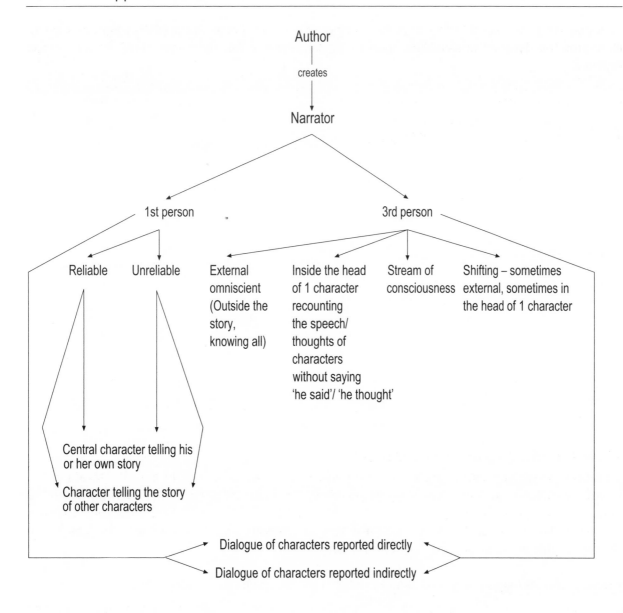

'The Murder' – from whose point of view?

In the activities on pages 23 and 24, you began to make some decisions about how you might tell your story, 'The Murder'.

- Use what you have learned in this unit to experiment with telling the story from different points of view. The diagram above summarises the possibilities you have to choose from. Remember, even if you decide to tell the story from the point of view of one character, you still have to decide whether you should write it in the first person or third person. How close do you want your reader to be to this character?

- Try writing a few paragraphs using different narrative viewpoints.

- Make a note of the effects you achieve writing the same story from different points of view.

- In whole class discussion, talk about your discoveries. What are the advantages and disadvantages of each approach?

Characters and characterisation

What is a character?

- In pairs, annotate the words in the boxes to explore the differences between 'person' and 'character' and between 'character' and 'characterisation'?

- Feed back your ideas in whole class discussion.

How are characters presented?

Because the writer's aim is usually to persuade the reader to believe in the characters in the novel, by making them as convincing as possible, it is often tempting to talk or write about the characters as if they were real people, with independent lives outside the boundaries of the plot. It is essential to remember that the characters are constructed by the writer who has made deliberate decisions about how to present them.

Some of the techniques a writer uses to present the characters are listed here.

- Description: by the narrator
   of appearance, personality, attitudes, behaviour

- Dialogue: what other characters say about them
   what they say
   how they speak

- Inner monologue

- Take responsibility for looking in detail at one of the characters in the novel you are studying. Identify the ways in which the writer has chosen to present this character and choose a short quotation to illustrate each technique.

- Take it in turns to present your analysis of each character.

- You could go on to repeat this exercise for a book of your own choice. Share what you discover with the rest of the class. Do different authors tend to use particular techniques?

The stars and the extras – classifying characters

In any novel some of the characters are more significant to the plot than others. These major characters are the most developed, or 'rounded'. These are the characters who change during the novel. The novelist and critic E.M. Forster described characters who are not as developed as 'flat'. 'Flat' characters, who play only a supporting role, are more predictable, behaving in similar ways whenever they appear.

- Sort the characters in the novel you are studying into two lists: major and minor. Sort them again, this time organising them into 'round' and 'flat' characters. Compare the two lists.

- Share your discoveries in whole class discussion.

- Use the list of characterisation techniques and your detailed work on individual characters to explore the ways in which the writer presents the major and the minor characters. Can you identify any patterns in the characterisation techniques used by the writer?

- How are the minor characters used by the writer? Do they fulfil a particular function? Use the functions suggested here to focus your discussion. Minor characters can be used:
  - to move the plot forward
  - to challenge ideas or provide a different point of view on events
  - to act as a foil to the main character, drawing attention to the similarities and differences between them
  - to represent an attitude or opinion
  - to illustrate a theme.

- Is it useful to think about the characters as being either 'flat' and minor or 'round' and major characters? What insights do you gain?

Your own writing – 'The Murder'
- Have a go at sketching in some of the characters for your seven sentence story. Choose a major character – perhaps the one from whose point of view the story is being told – and experiment with some of the techniques listed on page 28 to begin bringing them to life.

Characters and the reader
The reader's relationship with the main character, can affect his or her response to the whole novel.

- In pairs, talk about the statements listed here.

  - It is not possible to enjoy a book if you dislike the characters.
  - Readers need to identify with the main character.
  - Men cannot identify with a central character who is female.
  - Women can identify with characters who are male.
  - First person narrators are easier to identify with.
  - Novels written in the first person are more enjoyable.
  - Subject matter and style are unimportant compared with the characters.
  - There is a close relationship between the first person narrator, the writer and the reader.

- Use your thoughts on the statements to draft a paragraph outlining your own opinions on the relationship between the writer, the reader and the characters in the novel. Illustrate your ideas with examples from novels you have read.

Writing your own narrative

- Use everything you have learned in this section to write your own narrative (this may have to be a short story, rather than a novel, given the other demands on your time). Experiment with the following aspects of narrative, looking back at your notes and ideas to help you:
  - beginnings, middles and ends
  - handling time (narrative and chronological time)
  - narrative voice
  - different methods of characterisation.

You could make a conscious decision to echo or imitate the kinds of narrative choices made by the modern novelist you are studying. Alternatively, you could write, more freely, in your own style. Show a draft of your story to someone else – a friend, member of your class, teacher or other adult. Give them the chart below and ask them to fill it in for you as a 'response' sheet, to help you to re-draft the story.

	One aspect that worked well	One aspect that could be improved
Beginning		
Middle		
End		
Handling of Time		
Narrative Voice		
Characterisation		

- Re-draft your story.

- Write a commentary, explaining your choices, using the insights gained from the work you have done on the Modern Novel.

Enduring Love

by

Ian McEwan

A conversation

- In pairs, read the dialogue printed below and jot down your ideas about it. Use the prompts suggested here to help you focus your response.

  - What sort of conversation is it?
  - Where does it take place?
  - Who is it between?
  - What do you think might happen?
  - What else do you need to know?

- Choose short quotations to illustrate your ideas.

- Share your ideas with the rest of the class and talk about what else you need to know in order to make sense of it.

- Your teacher will give you some information about this dialogue to place it in context. At each stage make a note of how this information changes your response to the characters, the situation and your expectations of what might happen.

- Share your changing responses with the rest of the class and talk about your expectations of the novel from which this extract is taken.

> 'You'd better tell me what this is all about.'
> 'There's a coffee place ...'
> 'We'll be fine right here, I don't have a lot of time.'
> 'I'd rather we went inside.'
>
> 'Something's happened,'
> 'What's happened?'
> 'You know what it is,'
> 'Are we talking about the accident?'
> 'You know what it is, but you want me to say it.'
> 'I think you'd better. I have to go soon.'
> 'It's all about control, isn't it? It's so stupid to play games. Why don't you just say it. There's nothing to be ashamed of.'
>
> 'You think you're being cool about this, but it's ridiculous. You won't be able to keep it up, and you know it. Everything's changed now. Please don't put on this act. Please ...'
> 'You asked me to meet because you had something to say.'
> 'You're very cruel. But you've got all the power.'
>
> 'You love me. You love me, and there's nothing I can do but return your love.'
>
> 'I don't know why you've chosen me. All I know is that I love you too now, and that there's a reason for it, a purpose.'

Exploring the first chapter

Reading the opening paragraph

- Read the opening paragraphs of *Enduring Love* (up to 'I linger on our dispositions, the relative distances and the compass point – because as far as these occurrences were concerned, this was the last time I understood anything clearly at all.') On your own, make brief notes under the following headings:
  - what the extract is about
  - what the characters are like
  - narrative viewpoint
  - use of language (tone, particular word groups, metaphors)
  - the genre
  - references to what happens later
  - techniques to draw the reader in
  - what you are left wanting to know
  - your expectations of the novel.

Reader responses

The following quotations from other readers and reviewers of *Enduring Love* highlight the power of its opening chapter.

- Read the quotations and talk about how far they reflect your interpretation of the opening. Do any of them cause you to alter your own response?

> the first chapter ... makes an excellent short story
>
> the sense of the book is in the first chapter
>
> the first chapter is 'too wordy'
>
> Taut, compelling

In an interview Ian McEwan explained that one of his aims when writing *Enduring Love* was to make the opening like an 'addictive drug':

> I think it's possible to talk about a novel as a kind of building, and you're conducting the reader through its portals, through its entrance way. Those first impressions as you step into a building are crucial; openings are crucial. Getting someone to sit with your novel for eight or ten hours of their lives is a commitment, and somehow you've got to entice the reader into making that commitment. And I suppose I took this to something of an extreme in *Enduring Love.* So the story of the balloon became in a way that entrance hall. This is the first thing you see, and I hoped that I would write something that would have an addictive quality too. In fact, a couple of years later, I came across a couple of sentences in my notebook, in which I ordered myself to go and find an opening chapter to a novel that would be like an addictive drug, that once you started, you would be hooked.

Exploring chapter one

- Read the whole of the first chapter and talk about the ways in which McEwan tries to 'hook' the reader and draw him or her into the narrative. Some of the techniques he uses are suggested here:
  - dropping clues
  - holding back information
  - cliff hangers
  - slowing down the story – making the reader wait.

- Find examples of these techniques and any others that you notice.

Hooking the reader

Comparing first paragraphs

Printed below are the opening paragraphs from other novels and short stories by Ian McEwan.

- Read and annotate the extracts with your first responses to them.

- In pairs, share your ideas and talk about the following:
  - what you find interesting
  - whether or not they make you want to read on
  - what Ian McEwan seems to be doing in each case
  - the similarities and differences (for example, style, use of language, tone, relationship with the reader, key ideas or concerns).

1 I did not kill my father, but I sometimes felt I had helped him on his way. And but for the fact that it coincided with a landmark in my own physical growth, his death seemed insignificant compared with what followed. My sisters and I talked about him the week after he died, and Sue certainly cried when the ambulance men tucked him in a bright-red blanket and carried him away. He was a frail, irascible, obsessive man with yellowish hands and face. I am only including the little story of his death to explain how my sisters and I came to have such a large quantity of cement at our disposal.

The Cement Garden

2 Two former lovers of Molly Lane stood waiting outside the crematorium chapel with their backs to the February chill. It had all been said before, but they said it again.
'She never knew what hit her.'
'When she did it was too late.'
'Rapid onset.'
'Poor Molly.'
'Mmm.'
Poor Molly. It began with a tingling in her arm as she raised it outside the Dorchester Grill to stop a cab; a sensation that never went away. Within weeks she was fumbling for the names of things. *Parliament*, *chemistry*, *propeller* she could forgive herself, but less so *bed, cream, mirror*. It was after the temporary disappearance of *acanthus* and *bresaiola* that she sought medical advice, expecting reassurance. Instead, she was sent for tests, and in a sense, never returned.

Amsterdam

3 In Melton Mowbray in 1875 at an auction of articles of 'curiosity and worth', my great-grandfather, in the company of M his friend, bid for the penis of Captain Nicholls who died in Horsemonger jail in 1873. It was bottled in a glass twelve inches long, and noted my great-grandfather in his diary that night, 'in a beautiful state of preservation.' Also for auction was 'the unnamed portion of the late Lady Barrymore. It went to Sam Israels for fifty guineas.' My great-grandfather was keen on the idea of having the two items as a pair, and M dissuaded him. This illustrates perfectly their friendship. My great-grandfather the excitable theorist, M the man of action who knew when to bid at auctions.

from *First Love, Last Rites*

4 *... and for those parents, for too many years misguided by the pallid relativism of self-appointed childcare experts ...*
The Authorised Childcare Handbook, HMSO

Subsidising public transport had long been associated in the minds of both Government and the majority of its public with the denial of individual liberty. The various services collapsed twice a day at rush hour and it was quicker, Stephen found, to walk from his flat to Whitehall than to take a taxi. It was late May, barely nine-thirty, and already the temperature was nudging the eighties. He strode towards Vauxhall Bridge past double and treble files of trapped, throbbing cars, each with its solitary driver. In tone the pursuit of liberty was more resigned than passionate. Ringed fingers drummed patiently on the sill of a hot tin roof, white-shirted elbows poked through rolled-down windows. There were newspapers over steering wheels. Stephen stepped quickly through the crowds, through layers of in-car radio blather – jingles, high-energy breakfast DJs, newsflashes, traffic 'alerts'. Those drivers not reading listened stolidly. The steady forward press of the pavement crowds must have conveyed to them a sense of relative motion, of drifting slowly backwards. Jigging and weaving to overtake, Stephen remained as always, though barely consciously, on the watch for children, for a five-year-old girl. It was more than a habit, for a habit could be broken. This was a deep disposition, the outline experience had stencilled on character. It was not principally a search, though it had once been an obsessive hunt, and for a long time too. Two years on, only vestiges of that remained; now it was a longing, a dry hunger. There was a biological clock, dispassionate in its unstoppability, which let his daughter go on growing, extended and complicated her vocabulary, made her stronger, her movements surer.

The Child in Time

5 Ever since I lost mine in a road accident when I was eight, I have had my eye on other people's parents. This was particularly true during my teens when many of my friends were casting off their own folk, and I did rather well in a lonely, hand-me-down way. In our neighbourhood there was no shortage of faintly dejected fathers and mothers only too happy to have at least one seventeen-year-old around to appreciate their jokes, advice, cooking, even their money. At the same time I was something of a parent myself. My immediate milieu in those days was the new and disintegrating marriage of my sister Jean to a man called Harper. My protégée and intimate in this unhappy household was my three-year-old niece, Sally, Jean's only child. The rages and reconciliations that surged up and down the big apartment – Jean had inherited half the estate; my half was held in trust – tended to sweep Sally aside. Naturally, I identified with an abandoned child and so we holed up nicely from time to time in a large room overlooking the garden with her toys and my records, and a tiny kitchen we used whenever the savagery beyond made us not want to show our faces.

Black Dogs

Eight types of opening – Blake Morrison's categories

In the article printed on pages 19 and 20 of Section 1, Blake Morrison discusses the importance of the opening of a novel and suggests eight different types of first sentence.

- Use his suggestions to categorise the opening paragraphs you have just read.

    - Do any patterns emerge?
    - Are some approaches to the opening used more frequently than others?
    - Is this true of other contemporary novels you have read?
    - Is it true of pre-twentieth century novels?

- Take it in turns to feed back your ideas to the class.

- Look again at the opening sentence of *Enduring Love*. Which of the openings identified by Blake Morrison do you think describes it most accurately?

Writing creatively

- Write the opening paragraph of a novel either in the style of Ian McEwan or in one of the ways described by Blake Morrison.

- Take it in turns to read out your opening paragraphs. Which of Blake Morrison's categories would you place each one in?

Reading the novel

Strategies for a first reading

- Before you read *Enduring Love*, you might find it helpful to complete 'A personal reading profile' in section one of this pack and to talk about strategies for reading a novel.

- As you read the novel for a first time on your own, don't worry too much about anything you find puzzling. Use post-it notes to jot down questions or ideas and to identify any sections you would like to talk about in class.

- Suggestions for during reading activities are included in the Teachers' Notes on pages 73 and 74 of this pack.

The interview

You may find it helpful to watch the interview soon after your first reading of *Enduring Love*, before you go on to look more closely at key aspects of the novel. Alternatively, you could watch it at different stages during your first reading.

- After watching each section of the interview with Ian McEwan, talk in small groups, or as a whole class, about the questions suggested below.

1. Writing the novel (00:00:09)
- Make a note of the ideas and interests which McEwan suggests form the core of the novel. Talk about the way in which *Enduring Love* evolved and the ideas McEwan wanted to explore through the novel.

2. Narrative structure in the opening (00:03:52)
- Talk about McEwan's description of the novel's opening as a building.
  What insights do his decisions give you into the structure of the novel as a whole?
  Think about the opening chapter and talk about McEwan's suggestion that it is important to get the visual aspect of the novel right.

3. Establishing the character of Joe (00:07:21)
- Make brief notes on McEwan's description of Joe.
  Is McEwan's reading of Joe the same as yours? Is there anything about his analysis which you want to challenge or question?

4. The balloon dilemma (00:08:42)
- In your own words, explain what you now understand about evolutionary psychology.
  What role does McEwan see the balloon accident as playing in the novel?
  What insight does this contextual information give you into the novel (the storyline, the characters, relationships and so on)?

5. Playing with genre (00:10:43)

- List the reasons McEwan gives for using different genres in the novel.
  Skim through the novel and identify sections which you think are typical of the different
  genres he talks about.

6. Point of view and narrative voice (00:12:34)

- Make a note of McEwan's reasons for writing *Enduring Love* in the first person.
  In what ways does he suggest that Joe is an unreliable narrator?

7. Ideas and patterns – themes and the writer (00:16:40)

- Talk about what you think McEwan means when he says that 'as a novelist you are entering
  into a game … trying to think of the reader as a character in the novel.'
  What themes and patterns did you begin to notice on your first read through?

8. Love (00:17:57)

- What role does McEwan suggest love plays in the novel?
  What insight does this give you into the title?

9. Emotional versus rational (00:21:12)

- How does McEwan set up the opposition between the emotional and the rational?
  How is this opposition explored and challenged in the novel?

10. Science (00:24:27)

- What was McEwan attempting to do in writing about science in the form of a novel?
  Make a note of your ideas about the role science plays in the novel.

11. The endings (00:26:16)

- If you haven't done so already, note your response to the three endings of the novel.
  According to McEwan what is the purpose of each of these endings?

12. The modern novel (00:30:29)

- What does McEwan think characterises the modern novel? How far do you think these
  features are exemplified by *Enduring Love*? Look back at any work you completed from
  Section 1 of this pack and compare his ideas with your own.

Exploring genre

What sort of text is this?

- Read the following short extracts from *Enduring Love* and in groups talk about the ways in which they are similar and different.

- Working in groups, talk about the context in which you would normally expect to find this kind of writing and why. You should look closely at the style and language as well as the content to help you do this.

1 She was calm, and very angry. 'I've been sitting here half an hour, trying to tempt myself to open one of these drawers and take a look at your letters. And do you know, I couldn't raise the curiosity. Isn't that a terrible thing? I don't care about your secrets, and if you've got none, I don't care either. If you'd asked to see my letters I'd've said yes, go ahead. I've got nothing to hide from you.' Her voice rose a little and there was tremor in it too. I had never seen such fury in her before. 'You even left the drawer open so I'd know when I came in. It's a statement, a message, from you to me, it's a signal. The trouble is, I don't know what it means. Perhaps I'm being very stupid. So spell it out for me now, Joe. What is it you're trying to tell me?'

Page 132

2 The curving driveway brought us to a double garage built of cement blocks and painted an unevenly faded purple. Its rusting up-and-over door was padlocked. In front, poking through the long grass and the nettles were the skeletons and entrails of half a dozen motorbikes. It looked to me like a place where crimes could be safely committed. Running from an iron ring in the garage wall was a long chain with no dog on the end of it. This was where we stopped and got out. The nettles went right up to the Georgian front door. From the house came the sound of a bass guitar, a three-note figure fumblingly repeated.

'So where are the intellectuals?'

Johnny winced and made a downward pressing movement with his hand, as though to stuff my words back into a bottle. He spoke in a near-whisper as we approached the door. 'I'll give you some advice you might be grateful for. Don't make fun of these people. They haven't had your advantages, and they're, uh, not too stable.'

'You should have said. Let's go.' I pulled at Johnny's sleeve, but with his free hand he was ringing the bell.

'It's cool, he said, Just watch your step.'

I took a pace back and had half turned away, thinking I might walk off down the drive, when the door snapped open and habitual politeness constrained me. A powerful odour of burnt food and ammonia rolled, or blared, out of the house, momentarily silhouetting the figure who stood in the doorway.

'Johnny B. Well!' the man said. He had a shaved head and a small waxed moustache dyed with henna. 'What are you doing here?'

Page 192

3 Dear Joe, I feel happiness running through me like an electrical current. I close my eyes and see you as you were last night in the rain, across the road from me, with the unspoken love between us as strong as steel cable. I close my eyes and thank God out loud for letting you exist, for letting me exist in the same time and place as you, and for letting this strange adventure between us begin. I thank Him for every little thing about us. This morning I woke and on the wall beside my bed was a perfect disc of sunlight and I thanked Him for that same sunlight falling on you! Just as last night the rain that drenched you drenched me too and bound us. I praise God that He has sent me to you. I know there is difficulty and pain ahead of us, but the path that He sets us on is hard for a purpose. His purpose! It tests us and strengthens us, and in the long run it will bring us to even greater joy.'

Page 93

4   The high-velocity impact forced a fine spray, a blood mist, across our table-cloth, our desserts, our hands, our sight. My first impulse was simple and self-protective: I did not believe what I was seeing. Clichés are rooted in truth.

Page 172

5   The primitive, so-called sympathetic nervous system is a wondrous thing we share with all other species that owe their continued existence to being quick on the turn, fast and hard into battle, or fiery in flight. Evolution has culled us all into this efficiency. Nerve terminals buried deep in the tissue of the heart secrete their noradrenalin, and the heart lurches into accelerated pumping. More oxygen, more glucose, more energy, quicker thinking, stronger limbs. It's a system so ancient, developed so far back along the branchings of our mammalian and pre-mammalian past that its operations never penetrate into higher consciousness. There wouldn't be time anyway, and it wouldn't be efficient. We only get the effects. That shot to the heart appears to occur simultaneously with the perception of threat; even as the visual or auditory cortex is sorting and resolving into awareness what fell upon eye or ear, those potent droplets are falling.

Page 51

6   In 1942 de Clérambault carefully delineated the paradigm that bears his name, a syndrome he termed '*les psychoses passionelles*' or 'pure erotomania' to distinguish it from more generally accepted erotic paranoid states. The patient, or 'subject', usually a woman, has the intense delusional belief that a man, 'the object', often of higher social standing, is in love with her. The patient may have had little or no contact with the object of her delusion. The fact that the object is already married is likely to be regarded by the patient as irrelevant. His protestations of indifference or even hatred are seen as paradoxical or contradictory; her conviction that he 'really' loves her remains fixed. Other derived themes include beliefs that the object will never find true happiness without her, and also that the relationship is universally acknowledged and approved. De Clérambault was emphatic that in the pure form of the condition onset was precise and sudden, even explosive, and that this was an important differentiating factor; paranoid erotic states, he believed, probably erroneously (Enoch & Trethowan 1979), developed gradually.

Central to de Clérambault's paradigm was what he termed a 'fundamental postulate' of the patient having 'a conviction of being in amorous communication with a person of much higher rank, who has been the first to fall in love and was the first to make advances.' Such communication may take the form of secret signals, direct contact and the deployment of 'phenomenal resources' to meet the patient's needs. She feels she is watching over and protecting the object of her delusion …

Page 234

● At first glance, which, if any, of the extracts you have read could be described in the following ways?
  – a thriller
  – a book of ideas
  – a love story

- the tale of a terrifying stalking obsession
- a celebration of science and reason
- a warning about the limits of science and reason.

Playing with genre
The list above is how the official website for Ian McEwan describes *Enduring Love*.

Different readers and reviewers have highlighted the mix of genres as one of the most significant and interesting features of *Enduring Love*:

> The book reads on many different levels; it is a love story, a thriller, a horror and at times almost a psychological case study.

> *Enduring Love* gracefully bridges genres; it's a psychological thriller, a meditation on the narrative impulse, a novel of ideas.

- Add any other genres which you think McEwan uses in the novel. As a class, talk about why you think he decided to mix genres in this way.

- Listed below are key features and conventions of some of the different genres of writing which McEwan draws on in *Enduring Love*.

Thriller	**Detective story**	**Love story**
Novel is led by the plot Fast pace Suspense Dialogue and action Economical writing Characters often stereotypes Characters easily identifiable as 'goodies' or 'baddies' Settings can span the globe Chases Themes: political conspiracy, international crime, terrorism, innocents on the run, individuals suffering from psychosis Central figure normally male Hero isolated – 'going it alone' Not much emphasis on relationships Superficial sexual encounters	Element of puzzling over 'whodunnit' Plot led by the need to solve a crime Mystery Investigation Reader trying to solve the crime or mystery along with the 'hero' False clues Less action than in a thriller Reflection and commentary on events Stereotypical settings (for example, urban and gritty or country house and nostalgic)	Relationships lead the novel Focus on a few characters Narrowly focused settings Usually male/female relationships Often youthful, attractive main characters Much of the narrative is about what the characters are thinking or feeling Elements of vicarious sexual pleasure for the reader Obstacles threaten relationship (family, money, social class, infidelity, misunderstandings) Happy ending

- Look back at the extracts and identify short quotations which illustrate any of these features. Is there anything unexpected in the way McEwan uses features of these genres?

- Spend a few minutes sharing your discoveries with the rest of the class.

- Think back over your experience of reading the novel and make notes on the questions suggested here.

- Were you aware of the different genres as you read?
- Which of the different genres, styles or aspects of the novel were you most aware of?
- Which of the different genres, styles or aspects of the novel did you find most:
  interesting
  engaging
  challenging
  thought provoking
  memorable?
  Think about why this was.

● What, in your opinion is the effect of combining genres in this way?

In the interview Ian McEwan explains his decision to use different genres.

● Read what he has to say and compare his reasons with your own.

> I wanted a novel that would begin at a pace, at a lick. And, just as you might have a piece of music that starts furiously and then it might subside, by chapter 3 of *Enduring Love*, there is a kind of slowing down to get your breath for the new, the next wave of affliction to begin, which is Jed (Parry)'s obsession with Joe. In doing that, I'm quite consciously using the methods of a psychological thriller, or even the methods of a mainstream, Hollywood, psychological thriller, often opening on the run, on the hoof with a scene of some tension and some speed, in order then to pull back and start to patiently build a situation. I think literary novelists are always raiding other forms, for example science fiction. I also wrote a novel drawing heavily on the spy thriller conventions. The great attraction of it is that you can have fun up-ending the readers' expectations. The reason why these things are called genres, I think, is because they follow pretty cast iron rules. And the great thing about rules is, of course, that you can break them and have a little fun.

How the story is told

Writers' choices

Some of the choices writers are faced with when writing a novel are listed below.

● Read through these choices. Add any others you can think of.

- entirely chronological
- mainly chronological but with some flashbacks
- non-chronological
- one genre
- mix of genres
- description
- dialogue
- present tense
- past tense
- flashbacks
- one narrative perspective
- multiple perspective
- first person narrator
- third person narrator

● Read the following extract from the interview with Ian McEwan.

Enduring Love is one of those novels that started without any very clear intention whatsoever. Sometimes one begins projects like this. In fact, that section of the novel that has Joe Rose going off to get himself a gun was actually where I started. It was a way into a mass of material that was completely undigested at the time. I had no idea what I was doing, I simply thought well, I'm going to start somewhere, I want to get some writing going. It was almost like a five finger exercise. A man goes to get a gun, you write the episode, then you think, well, what does he want the gun for. At that point I connected with a great deal of reading that I'd been doing around science, and with some thinking I'd been doing about rationality and emotion, and how we think about these things, and how we incorporate them in our lives. This reading wasn't really directed towards any particular end – I was just following my curiosity. I've always had an interest in science. And it occurred to me that Joe was perhaps a scientist. And then later, I decided he'd be a science writer. I'd made notes years ago, four or five years back about my wish to write a kind of thriller, around which I would hang ideas. So there were ideas that I wanted to play with, and I thought the best way to do this would be to sugar the pill, and write a kind of thriller. At this point, I realised that I wanted a very rational fellow, like Joe Rose, a man who's got his life well sorted, who's happily married, who's very successful in his work, who takes a very rational approach to life. I wanted to put him through an ordeal. These elements came together rather haphazardly over the period of about a year.

I didn't come across my opening till I was maybe two thirds of the way through writing the novel. Up until that time, the opening of the novel had been precisely the scene in the restaurant, where an attempt is made on Joe's life. I thought that's the kind of fast moving thing I want, and I want to take it from the middle of the story. Then I heard about a ballooning accident in the South of Germany. As soon as I heard this scrap of a story, I had a clear idea of an opening, and that actually, I would begin this story at the beginning. When you're writing a scene with a lot of emotion in it, or a lot of drama in it, I think it is very important to get the visual aspect of it right. And I thought that a man like Joe, careful, patient, rational fellow that he is, would be very good at placing everything, giving you almost the points of the compass, how far things are away from each other, which direction he's running, where the wind is coming from. Everything placed just so, in order that the reader can have a clear view of it too. And in that way, I think the emotional relationships get sorted along the way. It also became part of Joe's characterisation: the way he tells this novel is that of a man who has a high regard for the orderly, the categorisable; the habits of clear and precise description remain with him. In some earlier draft of a novel that never got written, Joe is in fact a detective. Then I decided no, that was not going to work, and I was much happier to make him a science writer. It's always a major decision when you set out to write a novel to work out how it's going to be told. And, it's not simply a matter of telling it in the third person and playing God, or doing it autobiographically, as it were, in a pretend way, and telling it in the first person. There are all kinds of positions in between. And many third person narrations are, in fact, very limited, and become sort of over the shoulder forms of first person. And, in fact, with *Enduring Love*, I recast a couple of the chapters in the third person, on more than one occasion, just to get the taste of it, to see if I was doing the right thing.

- Talk about the decisions Ian McEwan made about how to tell the story, using the list of choices on page 43 to help you. You should think about how, and to what extent these decisions:
  - shape the novel
  - determine its meaning (for example, by placing emphasis on particular aspects)
  - affect its impact on the reader.

A focus on the first two chapters
- To help you think in more detail about the way the story is told, have a go at mapping the first two chapters of the novel. Make a chart, like the one shown here, showing the main events of the novel as they occur in narrative time. Then re-arrange the events in chronological order.

Narrative time	Chronological time

- Make brief notes on anything you find interesting or surprising about the way the story is told in these two chapters.

- Spend a few minutes sharing your ideas in class discussion. Is this pattern followed for the whole of the novel?

Exploring character

Introducing a character in role

- In pairs, take responsibility for working on one of the main characters. Collect together everything you know about them, for example:
  - facts about them
  - opinions and attitudes
  - interests
  - relationships with the other characters.

- Take it in turns to introduce your character to the class, in role. For instance, 'I'm Clarissa, Joe's partner and a university lecturer in English literature. I have recently been away from home for six weeks, doing some research on the letters of the poet, John Keats.'

Thinking about McEwan's presentation of your character

- Talk about the ways in which McEwan presents your character and the role he or she plays in the novel. Use the ideas on 'Character and characterisation' on page 28 to help you.

Tracing a response to the characters

- As a class, choose six key points in the novel. You could use the points suggested here:
  - the end of chapter 1
  - chapter 7
  - chapter 9
  - chapter 15
  - chapter 24 (the end of the main narrative)
  - appendix 1
  - the end of the novel.

- On your own, sketch a graph like the one shown here and trace your changing response to the main characters in the novel (Joe Rose, Clarissa, Jed, Jean Logan). Use a different colour pen for each character and indicate on a scale of 0-10 your sympathy for the character and the extent to which you trust his or her interpretation of events. What causes your response to change?

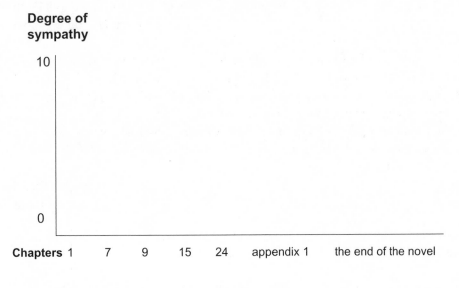

Degree of sympathy

10

0

Chapters 1   7   9   15   24   appendix 1   the end of the novel

0= No Sympathy   10 = Complete sympathy

- Compare your response with other people in the class.

- Jot down your ideas about the role each of these characters plays in the novel. What do they contribute in terms of plot, the exploration of ideas, the way the reader responds and so on?

- In pairs take responsibility for looking more closely at one of the characters. Make notes on the techniques McEwan uses to shape the response of the reader.

Writing about character

- Write a short paragraph on each of the three main characters (Joe, Clarissa and Jed), giving your personal response to the way McEwan presents them.

Other readers' responses to the characters

- Read the following comments about Joe, Clarissa and Jed and the role each plays in the novel. Jot down your response to each one.

1 Having the three central characters stand in for Science, the Arts and Religion is just lazy.

Reader reviews

2 Clarissa for all her grounded emotions and insights, has a lower status than, say, Julie in *The Child in Time*. McEwan's emotional engagement with feminism is less deferent than once it was.

Books Unlimited

3 But as we rush to the climax small jabs of doubt poke at us as we know more about the characters. Would Clarissa really react the way she does, given what we have learned about her? Would Joe and Clarissa's relationship really crumble so quickly? Are these moments of character revelation, or are they more in service of the plot dynamics?

Guardian Lit

4 Not only suspenseful, it is also thematically rich, opposing as it does Joe's scientific view of the world with that of Clarissa, a Keatsian scholar who believes, as the poet did, that science is robbing the world of wonder.

Science vs The Divine
The New York Times on the Web

5 McEwan makes Rose both thoroughly culpable and completely sympathetic. Parry's exotic illness is made credible by default. With Joe in charge of the narration, there's even a point where we wonder (with Clarissa) for a moment whether Jed might be the product of Rose's disturbed imagination.

The two names Joe and Jed, even suggest alter egos. Joe is, after all, disgusted with his job as popular science writer, recycling current materialisms into whatever shape pleases the public.

A genius for misery
(www.eyere.net)

- Discuss the interpretations, particularly the differences between those readers who praise McEwan's characterisation in the novel and those who are critical.

- To what extent do you agree with:
  - the reading of the character
  - the value judgements made?

These interpretations and criticisms of the characters in *Enduring Love* reveal some of the assumptions readers and reviewers have about novels in general and this one in particular. Some of these are suggested below.
- Well written characters are 'rounded' and believable.
- Characters should be realistic and behave like people do in real life.
- In novels characters are more important than ideas.
- A character should never be just a mouthpiece for an idea.
- A science writer is not a suitable narrator for a work of fiction.
- Anything a first person narrator says must be a reflection of what the author thinks.
- McEwan's decision to make Joe Rose a science writer was accidental and a mistake.

- Talk about these ideas in relation to *Enduring Love* and decide on your own view. Has anything you have read or talked about changed your response to the characters and the way McEwan presents them?

Characters' stories and interpretations

Seeing the world through different lenses

A key idea in the novel is that everyone has their own interpretation of any event. That interpretation is influenced by each individual's attitudes, beliefs and experiences. One reviewer commented that McEwan is interested in the ways 'we construct coherent narratives out of chaos'. McEwan explores this human characteristic through Joe, Clarissa, Jed and Jean Logan. Each character has a different 'take' on (or interpretation of) the balloon accident and tells their own story of what happened.

- Talk about what attitudes, beliefs and experiences have influenced each character's view of, and response to the accident.

- Find one short extract that reveals each character's interpretation of the event. For instance, on page 32 Joe says: 'Logan's death was pointless – that was part of the reason we were in shock. Good people sometimes suffered and died, not because their goodness was being tested, but precisely because there was nothing and no-one to test it.'

- What does the extract you have chosen reveal about the character's view of the world?

Joe, as a character, realises that every version of an event is a 'story'. He uses the language of storytelling to describe the way he tells his version of what happened. For instance, on page 29 of *Enduring Love*, he says, 'But this was unbearable too, so we returned to our own stories. Along the narrative lines there were knots, tangles of horror that we could not look at first time, but could only touch before retreating, and then return.'

- Look for some more examples of your own. You might focus particularly on the first three or four chapters.

Narrative viewpoints in the novel

First person or third person

- Look at the diagrams and notes on pages 25 and 27 of Section 1 to find out about the different points of view from which a story can be told. Talk about any books you have read or studied which use these different points of view. What do you think the advantages and disadvantages of each might be?

Using a first person narrator

In the interview Ian McEwan talks about his decision to use a first person narrator in *Enduring Love*.

> There's a long tradition in the novel, not only of a first person narrator, but the unreliable first person narrator. Here the novelist is involved in a kind of game with the reader. What you're doing is withholding information, or giving false information, because you have a pretend person, and you want your reader to enter into a relationship with this person. And just like a stranger on a train might regale you with a long story, and as you're nodding and humming, you're also asking to yourself is this story true, or how much of it is true, do I really believe this person, so with your first person narrator in fiction. As a writer, as a novelist, you are entering into a game, withholding the information, and trying to think of the reader as a character in the novel, trying to cast the reader as Clarissa or as the police, in order to give reality to this highly abstract quality which comes out of mere words on a page, which is a character.

Experimenting with the third person

During the writing of *Enduring Love*, Ian McEwan did experiment with writing some sections of the novel in the third person.

Printed below is a short extract from the opening chapter of the novel.

> The beginning is simple to mark. We were in sunlight under a turkey oak, partly protected from a strong, gusty wind. I was kneeling on the grass with a corkscrew in my hand, and Clarissa was passing me a bottle – a 1987 Daumas Gassac. This was the moment, this was the pinprick on the time map: I was stretching out my hand, and as the cool neck and the black foil touched my palm, we heard a man's shout. We turned to look across the field and saw the danger. Next thing, I was running towards it. The transformation was absolute: I don't recall dropping the corkscrew, or getting to my feet, or making a decision, or hearing the caution Clarissa called after me. What idiocy, to be racing into this story and its labyrinths, sprinting away from our happiness among the fresh spring grasses by the oak. There was the shout again, and a child's cry, enfeebled by the wind that roared in the tall trees along the hedgerows. I ran faster. And there, suddenly, from different points around the field, four other men were converging on the scene, running like me.

Page 1

- Have a go at re-writing the extract in the third person. As you do this, make a note of the following:
  - what you have to change
  - the difference it makes to the plot, the presentation of the characters, the impact of the scene
  - any difficulties you experienced.

- Take it in turns to read your versions of this episode to the rest of the class. Share your ideas about the difference it makes to tell the scene from this perspective, rather than from Joe's point of view. Why do you think McEwan decided to write the majority of the narrative in the first person?

Joe as narrator

Enduring Love is narrated in the first person by Joe.
- On your own jot down your ideas about the type of narrator he is. Choose three short extracts to illustrate your ideas and take it in turns to share these as a class.

- As a class, talk about why you think Ian McEwan chose to tell the story from the perspective of a character like Joe. What difference would it have made to tell the story still in the first person, but from Clarissa's point of view?

In the interview Ian McEwan explains his reasons for choosing to tell the story from the point of view of Joe, a scientist.

> When you're writing a scene with a lot of emotion in it or a lot of drama in it, it's very important to get the visual aspect of it right. And I thought that a man like Joe, careful, patient, rational fellow that he is, would be very good at placing everything ... in order that the reader can have a clear view of it too.

- Choose one or two passages where you think the style of the writing reflects the perspective of the narrator, Joe. Annotate this passage to show why you have chosen it and introduce it to the rest of the class.

Alternative viewpoints

One of the disadvantages of using a first person narrator is that the reader experiences only one character's interpretation of the events. They are also excluded from the thoughts of all the other characters. McEwan uses a number of narrative techniques to overcome this problem.
- Choose five different episodes in the novel where McEwan uses narrative 'voices' other than Joe's. Annotate the extracts to show how these 'voices' are developed and how they differ from Joe's 'voice'.

- Talk about what each 'voice' contributes to the plot, the ideas being explored and the reader's view of the characters.

- How else does McEwan remind the reader that they are only being told one version or interpretation of events?

A close focus on chapter 9

Chapter 9 is specially interesting and unusual in the way it uses voice and point of view.
- Re-read the opening paragraphs of this chapter and think about the questions suggested below.

  - What is interesting about the narrative perspective here?
  - Why do you think McEwan writes this section in this way?

    – What does it contribute to:
  • the reader's response to Joe
  • the reader's response to Clarissa
  • the key ideas of storytelling and interpretation?

Joe – an unreliable narrator

In first person narratives, readers may find it difficult to distinguish between the narrator and the author. It is easy to fall into the trap of thinking that what the narrator says must be what happened. Ian McEwan deliberately encourages the reader to doubt Joe Rose and his interpretation of events. This type of narrator is sometimes called 'an unreliable narrator'.

• Why do you think McEwan creates a character whom he wants the reader to question?

• Select a passage in which you, the reader, begin to doubt Joe's interpretation of the situation. Identify the ways in which McEwan manages to provoke this response.

• Share these as a group.

Joe himself is also aware of the impossibility of ever arriving at an objective, reliable version of the truth.

• Read the extract re-printed below and think about what it adds to your understanding of the key ideas of interpretation and unreliability, the characterisation of Joe, and his role in the novel.

> I felt a familiar disappointment. No one could agree on anything. We lived in a mist of half-shared, unreliable perception, and our sense data came warped by a prism of desire and belief, which tilted our memories too. We saw and remembered in our own favour and we persuaded ourselves along the way. Pitiless objectivity, especially about ourselves, was always a doomed social strategy. We're descended from the indignant, passionate tellers of half truths who in order to convince others, simultaneously convinced themselves ... And that was why metaphysics and science were such courageous enterprises, such startling inventions, bigger than the wheel, bigger than agriculture, human artifacts set right against the grain of human nature. Disinterested truth. But it couldn't save us from ourselves, the ruts were too deep. There could be no private redemption in objectivity.
>
> **Page 180**

Science in the novel

In the English & Media Centre interview Ian McEwan says, '*Enduring Love* is a novel that incorporates a great deal of science. As far as that goes, I would say that that has really been quite an important feature of contemporary writing'.

● To help you think more critically about the contribution played by science in *Enduring Love*, read these short extracts.

1   Those one or two ungrounded seconds occupy as much space in memory as might a long journey up an uncharted river. My first impulse was to hang on in order to keep the balloon weighted down. The child was incapable, and was about to be borne away. Two miles to the west were high-voltage power lines. A child alone and needing help. It was my duty to hang on, and I thought we would all do the same.
   Almost simultaneous with the desire to stay on the rope and save the boy, barely a neuronal pulse later, came other thoughts in which fear and instant calculations of logarithmic complexity were fused. We were rising, and the ground was dropping away as the balloon was pushed westwards …
   I didn't know, nor have I ever discovered, who let go first. I'm not prepared to accept that it was me. But everyone claims not to have been first. What is certain is that if we had not broken ranks, our collective weight would have brought the balloon to earth a quarter of the way down the slope a few seconds later as the gust subsided.

2   When there was movement across the room, I made a point of not looking up from my page even while I was taking nothing in. Then I gave way, and all I saw was a flash of a white shoe and something red, and the closing of the sighing swing doors that led out of the reading room on to the stairs …
   At that stage I still had not grasped the promptings of footwear and colour …

3   I tossed the pages on to the desk and as they landed I heard, for the second time that day, the creak of a floorboard behind me. There was someone at my back.

4   What was the explanation? Was she beginning to regret her life with me? Could she have met someone? If she wanted to leave me, she'd find it easier if she could convince herself that there was something between Parry and me. Had she met someone? At work? A colleague? A student?

● Now re-read the extracts in the immediate context in which they appear in the novel.

1   Those one or two ungrounded seconds occupy as much space in memory as might a long journey up an uncharted river. My first impulse was to hang on in order to keep the balloon weighted down. The child was incapable, and was about to be borne away. Two miles to the west were high-voltage power lines. A child alone and needing help. It was my duty to hang on, and I thought we would all do the same.
   Almost simultaneous with the desire to stay on the rope and save the boy, barely a neuronal pulse later, came other thoughts in which fear and instant calculations of logarithmic complexity were fused. We were rising, and the ground was dropping away as the balloon was pushed westwards …

I didn't know, nor have I ever discovered, who let go first. I'm not prepared to accept that it was me. But everyone claims not to have been first. What is certain is that if we had not broken ranks, our collective weight would have brought the balloon to earth a quarter of the way down the slope a few seconds later as the gust subsided. But as I've said, there was no team, there was no plan, no agreement to be broken. No failure. So can we accept that it was right, every man for himself? Were we all happy afterwards that this was a reasonable cause? We never had that comfort, for there was a deeper covenant, ancient and automatic, written in our nature. Co-operation – the basis of our earliest hunting successes, the force behind our evolving capacity for language, the glue of our social cohesion. Our misery in the aftermath was proof that we knew we had failed ourselves. But letting go was in our nature too. Selfishness is also written on our hearts. This is our mammalian conflict – what to give to others, and what to keep for yourself. Treading that line, keeping the others in check, and being kept in check by them, is what we call morality. Hanging a few feet above the Chilterns escarpment, our crew enacted morality's ancient, irresolvable dilemma: us, or me.

Someone said *me*, and then there was nothing to be gained by saying *us*. Mostly, we are good when it makes sense. A good society is one that makes sense of being good. Suddenly, hanging there below the basket, we were a bad society, we were disintegrating. Suddenly the sensible choice was to look out for yourself. The child was not my child, and I was not going to die for it. The moment I glimpsed a body fall away – but whose? – and I felt the balloon lurch upwards, the matter was settled; altruism had no place. Being good made no sense. I let go and fell, I reckon, about twelve feet. I landed heavily on my side and got away with a bruised thigh. Around me – before or after, I'm not so sure – bodies were thumping to the ground.

Page 13-15

2 When there was movement across the room, I made a point of not looking up from my page even while I was taking nothing in. Then I gave way, and all I saw was a flash of a white shoe and something red, and the closing of the sighing swing doors that led out of the reading room on to the stairs …

At that stage I still had not grasped the promptings of footwear and colour …

All day I'd been afraid. Was I so obtuse, not to know fear from the start? Wasn't it an elemental emotion, along with disgust, surprise, anger and elation, in Ekman's celebrated cross-cultural study? Was not fear and the recognition of it in others associated with neural activity in the amygdala, sunk deep in the old mammalian part of our brains from where it fired its instant responses?

Page 42-43

3 I tossed the pages on to the desk and as they landed I heard, for the second time that day, the creak of a floorboard behind me. There was someone at my back.

The primitive, so-called sympathetic nervous system is a wondrous thing we share with all other species that owe their continued existence to being quick on the turn, fast and hard into battle, or fiery in flight. Evolution has culled us all into this efficiency. Nerve terminals buried deep in the tissue of the heart secrete their noradrenalin, and the heart lurches into accelerated pumping. More oxygen, more glucose, more energy, quicker thinking, stronger limbs. It's a system so ancient, developed so far back along the branchings of our mammalian and pre-mammalian past that its operations never penetrate into higher consciousness. There wouldn't be time anyway, and it wouldn't be efficient. We only get the effects. That shot to the heart appears to occur simultaneously with the perception of threat; even as the visual or auditory cortex is sorting and resolving into awareness what fell upon eye or ear, those potent droplets are falling …

Page 51

4　What was the explanation? Was she beginning to regret her life with me? Could she have met someone? If she wanted to leave me, she'd find it easier if she could convince herself that there was something between Parry and me. Had she met someone? At work? A colleague? A student? Could this be an exemplary case of unacknowledged self-persuasion?

I got to my feet. Self-persuasion was a concept much loved by evolutionary psychologists. I had written a piece about it for an Australian magazine. It was pure armchair science, and it went like this: if you lived in a group, like humans have always done, persuading others of your own needs and interests would be fundamental to your well-being. Sometimes you had to use cunning. Clearly you would be at your most convincing if you persuaded yourself first and did not even have to pretend to believe what you were saying. The kind of self-deluding individuals who tended to do this flourished, as did their genes. So it was we squabbled and scrapped, for our unique intelligence was always at the service of our special pleading and selective blindness to the weaknesses of our case.

Page 103-104

- Talk about the difference it makes to your appreciation of the novel to read the scientific explanations of the characters' motivations. You should think about the following:
  - plot
  - character
  - the ideas being explored
  - the way in which you, as the reader, are encouraged to respond.

Listed below are some of the ways in which the science is included in the novel as a whole.
- Add any more you can think of and then choose extracts which exemplify each one. Make a note of what each contributes to the plot, the development of character and the exploration of ideas.

  - Joe's discussions with Clarissa
  - Joe's private thoughts and reflections
  - Joe's attempts to explain his own and others' behaviour
  - Joe's language
  - Jed's letter to Joe
  - The appendices

Writing about difficult ideas – evolutionary psychology and altruism

McEwan wanted to explore ideas to do with the way people behave and why. This is one of the main concerns of the new science of evolutionary psychology. He realised that to write about scientific ideas in a novel was a challenge.

Ideas are very difficult things in novels, they can really weigh a novel down, they can be very turgid, and perhaps the best way to write about your ideas is to write a philosophy book. So it's a curious matter, but still, there were ideas that I wanted to play with, and I thought the best way to do this would be to sugar the pill, and write a kind of thriller.

In this extract McEwan explains the basic ideas behind the new science of evolutionary psychology as they are explored in the context of *Enduring Love*.

Joe describes situations in terms of evolutionary psychology, which is one of his obsessions. When seven or eight, or six or seven people are hanging from a balloon, he describes it not simply in human or emotional terms, but in the terms of a man who is deeply involved with what we call biological thought. He wants to think not only what human nature is, but how it came about. As well as being hugely environmentally determined, we're also genetically determined, and these two rub off on each other in a close way. So, people hanging from a balloon have a simple drama to resolve amongst them. If they can all hang on together, they can bring the balloon to the ground. If someone breaks ranks, they obviously become collectively lighter, and then it makes sense to start thinking selfishly. And in that little drama, Joe sees, or I see through Joe, a kind of microcosm of human society. If we can hang together, as it were, and collaborate, everyone thrives. As soon as it breaks down, people have to start thinking for themselves, and you have collapse.

What Ian McEwan is saying here is based on evolutionary psychology. Evolutionary psychologists argue that just as our bodies have evolved, so have our minds. We have evolved to think and behave in a way which gives us the best chance of survival.

Are we always selfish? – a 5 minute debate
● Read the definition of altruism printed here.

> Altruism:
> – unselfish concern for others
> – behaviour of an animal that benefits others at its own expense.
> **Oxford Compact English Dictionary**

A key idea in evolutionary psychology is that no-one ever behaves in a wholly altruistic way.

● Spend a few minutes talking in pairs or threes about whether, based on your own experience of life, you think this is true. Does anyone ever behave in a way which will not benefit themselves?

● Hold a 5 minute debate in which you argue either for or against the claims of the evolutionary psychologists.

A scientific novel
The two short texts below and on page 55 are extracts from a radio debate with Melvyn Bragg and *The Moral Animal* by Robert Wright – a text recommended by Ian McEwan. They discuss ideas about evolution, evolutionary psychology and altruism in more detail.

● Read the extracts and, as a class, talk about the central ideas.

● Working together, highlight ideas and arguments which seem to you to be relevant to the ideas debated by Joe Rose and explored through the story of *Enduring Love*.

● Identify a passage from the novel which considers the ideas discussed here. Explain how you think McEwan is making use of the scientific ideas in the passage you have chosen.

The Darwin Debate with Melvyn Bragg
Bragg: I mean, does evolutionary theory have anything to say about altruism or tenderness or morality?

Meredith Small: Sure but at a group level, a population level rather than an individual level – not why is John or Mary an altruist, but why people are sometimes altruistic, you can ask it that.

Bragg: And you think there's an evolutionary answer for that?

Small: No, not really. Everyone always says humans are the only species that are altruistic but if you look at the cases of altruism they're incredibly rare – the man jumping into the river to save people after a plane crash. That's why they're in the news because they're incredibly rare. And usually when people are altruistic at some level they're receiving something back, so it's not true altruism, even if it's the emotional satisfaction of helping someone out.

Bragg: And evolutionary theory in that respect has nothing to tell us about morality you think?

Small: I think it probably does. Hans de Val has written at great length about the biological basis of morality, suggesting again that chimpanzees, other primates, other social animals have the same systems that we do in terms of justice and empathy and that there may be a biological basis for right and wrong, knowing right and wrong and punishment for wrong and rewarding right behaviour in a social situation.

(www.bbc.co.uk/education/darwin/debate/transcript.html)

The Moral Animal

Altruism, compassion, empathy, love, conscience, the sense of justice – all of these things, the things that hold society together, the things that allow our species to think so highly of itself, can now confidently be said to have a firm genetic basis. That's the good news. The bad news is that, although these things are in some ways blessings for humanity as a whole, they didn't evolve for the 'good of the species' and aren't reliably employed to that end. Quite the contrary: it is now clearer than ever how (and precisely *why*) the moral sentiments are used with brutal flexibility, switched on and off in keeping with self-interest; and how naturally oblivious we often are to this switching. In this new view, human beings are a species splendid in their array of moral equipment, tragic in their propensity to misuse it, and pathetic in their constitutional ignorance of the misuse.

Deception and self deception

Reciprocal altruism brings its own agenda to the presentation of self, and thus to the deception of self. Whereas status hierarchies place a premium on our seeming competent, attractive, strong, smart, etcetera, reciprocal altruism puts its accent on niceness, integrity, fairness. These are things that make us seem like worthy reciprocal altruists. They make people want to strike up a relationship with us. Puffing up our reputations as decent and generous folk can't hurt, and it often helps.

Richard Alexander, in particular, has stressed the evolutionary importance of moral self-advertisement. In *The Biology of Moral Systems* he writes that 'modern society is filled with myths' about our goodness: 'that scientists are humble and devoted truth-seekers; that doctors dedicate their lives to the alleviation of suffering; that teachers dedicate their lives to their students; that we are all basically law abiding, kind, altruistic souls who place everyone's interest before their own.'

There's no reason moral self-inflation has to involve self-deception. But there's little doubt that it can ...

Our repertoire of moral excuses is large. Psychologists have found that people justify their failure to help others by minimizing, variously, the person's plight, their own responsibility for the plight, and their own competence to help.

Robert Wright

- Read the statements below in pairs or as a class and spend a few minutes talking about each one. Decide whether or not you agree with them and make a note of your reasons.

  – In *Enduring Love*, Ian McEwan successfully incorporates science into a novel.
  – The science weighs heavily in *Enduring Love*.
  – You need to understand evolutionary psychology to fully appreciate the novel.
  – Without the science, *Enduring Love* would be a very light read.
  – By including scientific ideas in *Enduring Love*, Ian McEwan is using the form of the novel to do something new.
  – *Enduring Love* helps you to understand difficult scientific ideas.
  – You don't need to know anything about science to enjoy this book.
  – Without the science, *Enduring Love* would be a great read.

Other readers' responses to the science in the novel

Printed below are a selection of quotations from other readers.
- Consider each one in turn and choose:
  – one you agree with or which causes you to re-think your interpretation
  – one with which you disagree.

Write a paragraph responding in some detail to each of these readings, using the text to illustrate your argument.

1 Strong on suggesting the fine line between sanity and its alternative, this is also a neat spin on the science vs religion debate. No, it's not subtle, the symbols are not hidden, and yes, the Jed character is underdeveloped, but surely this is about the mental wrestling match Joe is having with his own contradictions.

Reader reviews

2 As for science vs religion, this debate is never organic to the book.

Reader reviews (Amazon.co.uk)

3 The science [is] clearly a tool for eventually talking about the syndrome on which the book hinges.

Reader reviews (Amazon.co.uk)

4 The end intrigues me and the lines between truth as exemplified by science – and fiction (or faith) are very blurred.

Reader reviews (Amazon.co.uk)

5 He is the master at creating suspense: the particular sickening, seesawing kind that demands a kind of physical courage from the reader to continue reading. McEwan will rise higher, though, if he lets go of the half-baked ideas.

New Statesman

6 Novelists should tell us stories, not relate particle physics. I'm all in favour of the novel of ideas, but at least let the ideas be the author's own. An author's individuality is drowned in this sea of science.

Literary Review

7   He covers some of the territory familiar to his readers: obsession and its consequences, violent events, moral dilemmas.

Reader review

8   If the science is the least convincing element then its core, the devastating effect of obsession on normality, the power of pathological love against the merely loving, is never in doubt ... At the end come several appendices ... This is a mildly disappointing way to finish such a fine book (when does the post modern begin to look quaint?).

Reader review

9   Most frustrating is the amount of science written about which is clearly a tool for eventually talking about the syndrome on which the book hinges. The talk of hubble telescopes and Darwinian theories, while interesting, are irritatingly out of place.

Reader review

A question of endings

The final chapter of *Enduring Love* is not the end of the novel. Although Joe Rose's narrative has ended, the novel has not. The account of the picnic is followed by two appendices: the case study and a letter from Jed.

- Read each of the endings and talk about why you think McEwan chose to delay the novel's 'closure' in this way. What does each ending contribute to your understanding and appreciation of the novel and of the ideas it raises (for example, the attempt to make sense of, or impose order on different experiences)? How does each ending alter your response to what you have just read?

The appendices

Although de Clérambault's syndrome is a real, psychiatric illness, the case study in the appendix is based on the novel. The detailed discussion of the condition was also written by McEwan.

- Read this medical definition of de Clérambault's syndrome and talk about how McEwan has used both this illness and the style and conventions of the medical report in his novel. Why do you think McEwan chose to put the information about de Clérambault at the end rather than integrate it into the narrative, perhaps as an article discovered by Joe Rose?

> **Erotomania**
>
> De Clérambault's Syndrome, is a mental state characterised by the delusion that the sufferer is passionately loved by another – usually a public figure or slight acquaintance. The object of the erotomanic individual's affections is frequently unaware of this delusion and has done nothing to encourage it; simultaneously, the erotomaniac believes that the victim was the first to fall in love and make the initial advances, and that they are in a mutually-desired amorous relationship. Delusions often include the interpretation of *innocent, everyday gestures* by the victim as *secret messages of love*. Erotomanic delusions are typically extremely robust; however, a sequence of rejected advances will eventually frustrate the sufferer, who may then become violent towards his or her *victim*.
>
> **(www.members.fortunecity.com/squabmaster/erotomania.html)**

Readers' responses to the case studies

Many people, including members of the British Institute of Psychiatry, assumed that the case study was genuine and that this was the origin of the novel.
- Read the following comments on the appendices and on McEwan's use of de Clérambault's syndrome in the novel. Use the questions suggested here as the starting point for your discussion.

  - What difference does a reader's interpretation of this appendix make to their response to the novel as a whole?
  - If the story were based on a genuine case study, would this make it more or less of an achievement as a novel?
  - What do the comments suggest about the reader's expectations of, and assumptions about 'the novel'?

- Do you agree with the judgements these readers make?

Grand Delusion

Unless the appendix is an elaborate fiction, ... then we finally have to assume that McEwan is quoting an actual case history and modelling the events of the novel closely upon it. It is an impressive transformation, the rearing up of a fictional world around summary notations from the realm of the actual.

Sven Birkerts, *New York Times on the Web*, 25 January 1998

A convincing fiction

Does de Clérambault's syndrome really exist? Or is this a convincing fiction that most people seem to be accepting as truth because it is wrapped up in the rubric of scientific relevance. Just as there is a tendency for people to believe statistics because they involve numbers, this might be the new 'faith' of our culture. Unless people are prepared to question any 'science' which is put before them, they are equally at risk as believing the more extreme interpretations of religion.

Reader review

Mistaken interpretations of the case study

The article printed here recounts the mistaken assumptions made about the appendices and their relationship to the rest of the novel. In it McEwan also makes some more general comments about the relationship between fact and fiction, real people and imaginary characters, the process of storytelling and the means by which we make sense of our lives.

- Read the article and talk about the issues McEwan raises about fiction, the role of the writer and the place of the novel in modern life.

- Does it matter whether we read the case study as fact or fiction? If so, why?

Fooled You

The saga began in 1997 with the publication of McEwan's acclaimed novel *Enduring Love*, the story of a science journalist, Joe Rose, obsessively and violently stalked by a religious loner called Jed Parry. Joe diagnoses Jed's condition as a homoerotic manifestation of De Clérambault's Syndrome, a nightmarish state of 'erotomania' named after the turn-of-the-century French psychiatrist who first identified it.

It's a compelling, deeply disturbing tale – and one rendered even more haunting by the presence in the book's appendix of a case report reprinted from the British Review of Psychiatry, by Drs Robert Wenn and Antonio Camia, detailing the terrifying real-life case on which the story is based.

Only it isn't. The British Review of Psychiatry doesn't exist. And the paper – despite its authentic footnotes and expert grasp of the psychiatric lexicon ... is McEwan's invention. ...

'I can confirm that Appendix 1 of *Enduring Love* is fictional, based on the novel that precedes it rather than the other way around ... If the monograph had been published, it would have seemed that my novel was based on a genuine case, my characters would have acquired an extra sheen of plausibility and the division between the real and invented world would have become seamless. ...

It's always very tempting for a writer to blur the line between fiction and reality. It gives the fiction an added authority and unsettles the factual. And it was linguistic exuberance, as well ...'

We should be wary, he warns, of drawing too clear a distinction between the world of the fictional and that of the psychiatric report.

'Psychiatric case studies are like small novels ... To base a psychiatric theory on what one person says he or she discovered of another person is fantastically unscientific and owes much to a certain kind of literary interpolation. So why not go the whole way? Why not subject the characters in your novel to psychiatric study?'

Oliver Burkeman, *The Guardian*, 16 August 1999

Ideas and patterns

The role of the reader

In the interview McEwan says:

> Themes are what readers have to address, rather than writers. You're dealing, as a writer, with generating a reality out of these scraps, and they come together in a haphazard way. And slowly, over months, or a year, or two or three years, you impose a kind of order, so that you have an intact world. And then you discover that you've addressed certain matters, and that they repeat themselves throughout, not necessarily in line with your intentions.

However, he does acknowledge that he was particularly interested in exploring ideas such as rationality and the new science of evolutionary psychology.

- You are now in a position to think back over your reading of *Enduring Love*. What ideas and issues do you think Ian McEwan has addressed? Which ideas and issues particularly interested you? Choose one to talk about briefly to the rest of the group.

Exploring oppositions

One way to read *Enduring Love* is as an exploration of oppositions. The situation McEwan develops places these oppositions in tension and subjects them to extreme pressure.

Exploring oppositions

- In pairs or small groups, take responsibility for looking in more detail at one of the oppositions listed below. Talk about the ways in which this opposition is explored in the novel, for example through the plot, Joe's thoughts, conversations, the letters, the characters and so on. Which character(s) do you associate with these ideas, beliefs or attitudes? Choose key quotations to illustrate your ideas and present your work as a display. Take it in turns to feed back your ideas to the rest of the class.

  - Rationality v emotion
  - Science v imagination
  - Religion v science
  - Faith v evidence
  - Belief v scepticism
  - Abnormal v normal behaviour
  - Individualism v society (me and us)
  - The individual perspective v the big picture
  - Fact v story
  - Truth v fiction
  - Male v female
  - Love v hatred
  - Homosexual v heterosexual

- Share your ideas as a class.

- Read the interpretations listed below and use them to help you focus your own reading of the oppositions in *Enduring Love*.

  - In *Enduring Love* oppositions are established but no conclusion is reached as to which is better.
  - Of each pair of oppositions, one is shown to be 'right'.
  - In *Enduring Love* Ian McEwan sets up a series of oppositions and then deconstructs them, suggesting that they are not mutually exclusive.

- Talk about how helpful it is to analyse the novel in this way. What insights does an awareness of these patterns provoke? Which aspects of the novel do you think are marginalised by this kind of reading (for example, character or the response of the reader)?

- Read the following quotation and compare the oppositions identified here with your list.

> Religion versus rationality. Your memory versus mine. Love versus daily existence. Sacrificing an individual for the good of the masses.
>
> In McEwan's works, the opposite is a theme. His characters may take action that seems opposite to all sorts of things, their best interests, their lovers, their friends, their morals, or their political, religious or rationalist beliefs. This is the tension and the story.
>
> **from *The Random House Reading Group Guide* on Ian McEwan**

Enduring Love in context

The science/arts divide

- Spend a few minutes talking together about your views about science and the arts or humanities. Use the prompts suggested here to focus your thinking:
  - your image of a scientist
  - your image of an artist
  - your impression of the way science and scientists are presented in newspapers, on the radio and television, in film
  - your impression of the way artists, writers and 'creative' subjects are presented in newspapers, on the radio and television, in film
  - issues about combining A Level in English Literature with other arts subjects or with science subjects.

One of Joe's concerns in *Enduring Love* is the way in which, during the twentieth century, science and the arts have becoming increasingly specialised and separate.

> It was the nineteenth-century culture of the amateur that nourished the anecdotal scientist. All those gentleman without careers, those parsons with time to burn. Darwin himself, in pre-*Beagle* days, dreamed of a country living where he could pursue his collector's passion, and even in the life that genius and passion got him, Downe House was more parsonage than laboratory. The dominant artistic form was the novel, great sprawling narratives which not only charted private fates, but made whole societies in mirror image and addressed the public issues of the day. Most educated people read contemporary novels. Storytelling was deep in the nineteenth-century soul.
>
> Then two things happened. Science became more difficult, and it became more professionalised. It moved into the universities, parsonical narratives gave way to hard-edged theories that could survive intact without experimental support and which had their own formal aesthetic. At the same time, in literature and in other arts, a newfangled modernism celebrated formal, structural qualities, inner coherence and self-reference. A priesthood guarded the temples of this difficult art against the trespasses of the common man.
>
> Likewise in science.
>
> **Page 48**

- Talk about the issues raised in this extract. Think particularly about them in the context of the novel and McEwan's decision to use fiction to explore ideas more usually encountered in a science book.

Enduring Love does not exist in a vacuum. The issues raised by Joe, and McEwan's decision to explore scientific theories in a novel, contribute to a wider debate about the relationship between science and the arts. The extracts printed below comment on, and explore, the changing relationship between the sciences and the arts.

- Read the extracts. Make a note of the main arguments by the different commentators and jot down your own response to the points they make.

Science for the general reader

Those readers of *Enduring Love* who do have a curiosity about science would do well to look at some of those books I've mentioned in the acknowledgements at the back. I think we've lived through, and are living through a very, very good time for science writing. Really good, articulate, literate scientists are writing about their fields for the general readership, in ways that I think were not available twenty years ago. A number of journalists, non scientists, have found ways of writing about science which are very involving and, again, well written. So at the back of *Enduring Love* does lie this marvellous, relatively fresh field of science writing, of which Joe himself is an acting participant. It's subject to fashions – the dinosaurs replaced by black holes, replaced by neo Darwinism, and so on, but for all that a real golden age. And I've benefited from that, profited from that enormously.

Ian McEwan

Whose side are you on?

Scientists rule OK? Certainly, they seem wholly and comfortably embedded in the culture, envied for their grip on the steering wheel of the times. Surely, finally it is the dawning of the Age of Einstein's children. Yet this recent trend appears only after years of a widely acknowledged rift between the arts and the sciences that has always been to the disadvantage of the scientists. This new love-affair may be no more than mere fashion, papering over the chasm described 40 years ago by a tall, short-sighted novelist who had been trained as a scientist.

Charles Percy Snow delivered The Rede Lecture and called it: 'The Two Cultures and the Scientific Revolution' in 1959 ... Snow's ideas were not original but his lecture hit the nerve of the obvious. And for much of the time since then we have lived in the Cold War of intellectual confrontation, arts and sciences mutually deterrent, walled against each other ...

But, is Snow still right about the split between the cultures? When Pinker, Dawkins, Hawking, Greenfield and so many others have seized the central arguments even in the most literary journals; when Michael Frayn and Tom Stoppard put on West End plays about chaos theory and the uncertainty principle, and novelists such as Douglas Adams and Ian McEwan chew scientific fat in their fiction; when over the past few years world-class scientists come on to Radio 4 talk programmes hitherto dominated by showbusiness and arts folk and engage with substantial audiences ... have not the walls fallen? Genes are the talk of the town, the Big Bang is in every Christmas cracker. Darwin and DNA stalk the supermarket. Scientists fill the lecture halls ...

A key factor, I believe, still driving a wedge between the two cultures, has been the ascription of the Imagination to the arts only, leaving science as the PC Plod of dull thought.

Melvyn Bragg

The context of science fictions – wider reading

Until recently science only came into novels as science fiction – a novelist's prediction or fantasy of what science in the future or in another world might be like. Famous examples include: *Frankenstein* by Mary Shelley; *Brave New World* by Aldous Huxley; *The Time Machine* by H.G. Wells; *Dr. Jekyll and Mr Hyde* by Robert Louis Stevenson and the *Foundation* trilogy by Isaac Asimov. At the end of the twentieth century, writers of fiction began to explore science *fact* in their novels. At the same time writers of popular science began to use the techniques of the novelists. Some of these books are listed here.

Fiction and drama: *Mendel's Dwarf* by Simon Euwer; *Mrs Einstein* by Anna McGrail; *Arcadia* by Tom Stoppard and *Copenhagen* by Michael Frayn.
Non-fiction: *Genome* by Matt Ridley and *Longitude* by Dava Sobel.

- Take responsibility for reading or dipping into one of these and prepare a brief report on it. You should think about the following:
  - the relationship between the scientific ideas and the contexts in which these are explored

(for example, the genre used)
- the language
- the style and tone
- the relationship with the reader
- the ways it is similar to, and different from *Enduring Love*
- the difference it makes to read *Enduring Love* in the context of this other contemporary writing.

The context of the modern novel

The extracts below are about the modern novel at the end of the twentieth century.

- Read the extracts and pick out the main points and arguments in each one. How do these arguments fit with your experience of reading *Enduring Love*?

1

Is the novel dead?

The last decade has seen the rise and rise of the non-fiction best seller ... In the face of the rampant success of such a broad range of non-fiction ... is there any truth in Peter Ackroyd's assertion that the novel is dead? Well, no is the brief answer ... But something very peculiar is definitely happening. Novelists are more and more writing about historical characters or situations, whilst non-fiction writers are using the methods of the novelists for their narratives ... Successful non-fiction writers are as interested in characterisation, narrative flow, point of view and all the other tricks of the novelist's trade as writers of fiction are.

Indeed, sometimes the line between truth and fiction blurs ...

There's no reason why non-fiction narratives of all sorts shouldn't continue to increase in popularity. Many of the historical narratives have a scientific bent and science is increasingly popular as we approach the millennium.

Peter Guttridge

2

Searching For England

If an English novelist writes realistically about the present the result is usually banal, uninteresting or reads like a style piece. For some strange cultural reason when, say, Saul Bellow writes about a professor in Chicago you feel he is going to take the temperature of the soul of modern man. If an English novelist does the same, you feel it is either going to be a campus novel or an embarrassment. Something in our culture is self-mocking.

Professor Lola Young, chair of the Orange Prize judges, complained of the 'piffling and parochial' nature of English fiction when explaining why her shortlist was dominated by North Americans ...

Pankaj Mishra, the young Indian writer says 'The American comparison is unfair.' 'America is an immigrant society, the immigrant experience keeps producing new writers, and so it follows that Chicago with its new arrivals continues to be more interesting. England was an imperial society, and now it is just another one of the consumerist societies of the west. The density and range of social experience that was available to the 19th century English novelist – and is still available to the immigrant writer in America – doesn't exist for the contemporary English novelist.'

Mishra – along with V.S.Naipaul to whom I spoke – believes that the English writer's relationship with society has fundamentally altered. He has lost his interpretative role. Fiction has ceased to be an act of moral inquiry, a mechanism by which to discover the honest truths about individual lives and societies, and has become an entertainment, a diversion. 'There was a time,' Naipaul says, 'when fiction provided discoveries about the nature of society, about states, which gave those works a validity over and above the narrative element. That's gone.'

Jason Cowley, *W*, the Waterstone's magazine (Summer/Autumn 1999)

Interpretations by other readers

Readers' 'sound-bite' responses

- Read the quotations below, taken from reviews of *Enduring Love*.

- Choose one as the starting point for a 'just-a-minute' unscripted comment on the novel, in front of the class. You could either develop the comment or argue against it, for example: '*Enduring Love* is an intellectual potboiler' – I completely disagree. It is far more sophisticated and subtly written than this comment suggests.'

1   A horrifying if thematically lush tale of obsession, guilt, disillusion, distrust, psychosis and the erosion and perversion of love.

2   McEwan's writing is unflaggingly poised.

3   McEwan is capable of excavating deep, painful trenches in the back corridors of the psyche and the heart.

4   *Enduring Love* forces us to confront the insidious creepiness of life.

5   *Enduring Love* raises some big questions about evil and goodness, blame and forgiveness, science and art.

6   *Enduring Love* is an intellectual potboiler.

7   *Enduring Love* has all the elements of a good mystery or crime thriller.

8   The book starts with a scenario straight out of an undergraduate ethics course.

9   The stalking of Rose becomes an excruciating reading experience.

10   The climaxes in his fiction have an eerie inertia.

11   This is the writer as stalker, agent and patient in a delusional system that bestows anxiety to the very last page.

12   The novel would have been deeper and stronger for being more impartial and less schematic.

Reviewers' responses to *Enduring Love*

- Read the reviews that follow, annotating them to show your response to the interpretations and assumptions made by the reviewer.

- Make a list of the interpretations you agree with and those you disagree with. Choose a couple of the points you disagree with most strongly and write brief notes arguing the case for your interpretation.

- Identify any interpretations which make you re-consider your own reading of the novel. How is your reading shaped by reading the novel in the context of the interpretations by other readers?

- In pairs, take responsibility for looking in more detail at the way one of the reviews is written. Use the questions suggested here to help you.

  - What is the critic is most interested in (e.g. character, plot, narrative technique, reader responses, contextual issues and so on)?
  - What expectations and assumptions does the critic have about novels in general and *Enduring Love* in particular (for example, what is a suitable subject for novels, the relationship between the narrator and the writer)?
  - To what extent is the critic describing, analysing or evaluating the novel?
  - What kind of audience is suggested by the tone, length and focus of the review?
  - What does the review reveal about the reviewer's expectations of the novel as a genre?
  - To what extent do you agree with what the reviewer is saying?

- Write a detailed response to one of the reviews, in which you explore how it works as a piece of critical writing, as well as commenting in detail on the arguments it raises about the novel. Use evidence from both the review and the novel in your analysis.

Review 1 Over-fished Waters

The condition which McEwan describes is, apparently, a real one. De Clérambault's Syndrome was named after the French doctor who first identified the disorder when he treated a woman who was convinced that George V (whom she had never met) was in love with her. She would stand outside Buckingham Palace for hours at a time, believing that the king was communicating with her by drawing the curtains.

What makes McEwan's depiction of the illness so compelling – and so alarming – is how close it seems to ordinary romantic attachment. The letters that Jed writes to Joe are like real love letters; his entreaties would be familiar to anyone who has suffered from unrequited love. It is, in fact, when Jed's behaviour is closest to what passes for normal that his presence induces the most queasy discomfort. Once he topples into Hitchcockian melodrama he becomes more ridiculous than threatening. Even his proxy attempt on Joe's life strains for credence: no self respecting team of hired assassins would fire a gun in a crowded West End restaurant at lunch time, when the victim's home address is freely available.

The violent excesses of De Clérmabault's would be enough for most novelists, but not Ian McEwan. There is a subplot involving the widow of the man killed in the ballooning accident, and Joe's troubled relationship with Clarissa is another central part of the book. Then there is a detailed description of Clarissa's academic work on Keats, set against the rationalism of Joe's scientific investigations. The book burgeons with coincidence, events and ideas: it's like getting three novels for the price of one.

As well as its excellent story, *Enduring Love* is a worthwhile attempt to view the irrational through the lens of the rational. But it is weighed down by a surfeit of scientific information.

As a result I would now like to use these pages to call for an immediate, worldwide moratorium on novelists reading works of science. Like oceans plundered of whales, science books have become over-fished by voracious, imaginative writers. You can't pick up a novel these days without being bombarded by Heisenberg's Uncertainty Principle, or the latest theories on Darwinism. Popular science now occupies ample shelf-room in every bookshop and a prominent place in best-seller lists. Novelists should tell us stories, not recite particle physics. I'm all in favour of the novel of ideas, but at least let the ideas be the author's own. An author's individuality is drowned in this sea of science. Much as I enjoyed *Enduring Love*, I missed Ian McEwan.

Cressida Connolly

Review 2 I think I'm right, therefore I am

It speaks well for Ian McEwan's descriptive powers and the fluency of his invention that this opening scene doesn't smell like essence of quandary, a carefully contrived human theorem, although his choice of profession for Joe a popularising science writer makes his mouthpiece almost too exquisitely adept at analysing its implications: 'This is our mammalian conflict what to give to others, and what to keep for yourself.' This, though, is the novel's painful point, as shown by the repercussions of the tragedy, that knowing more about the factors that determine your behaviour is not the same thing as becoming either freer or wiser ...

Rationality is a precious and precarious construct in the novel, not an instinct but an achievement, a sandcastle no sooner built than washed away by the tides of the mind. The woman widowed in the accident turns out, when Joe contacts her (to exorcise his sense of guilt) to have an obsession of her own. She is convinced that her husband, a notably cautious man, must have been trying to impress someone and therefore, inevitably, a lover unseen by the others when he held on to the rope too fatally long ...

The collapse of a couple under pressure is a recurrent McEwan theme ... The couple is the smallest possible viable society; the breakdown between Joe and Clarissa is the subtlest variation yet on the theme. A lovingly maintained fabric that seemed to have no dangling threads unravels thoroughly.

This relationship is part of what is referred to in the title, but there is also 'enduring', in the sense of being on the receiving end of, as Joe is of Parry's mystical love. Joe makes sense of Parry's infatuation by classifying it as an instance of the pathological condition, 'de Clérambault's syndrome', one of whose peculiarities is, ironically, that it can last indefinitely, since it isn't dependent on reciprocation ... Joe wants to see this syndrome as 'a dark, distorting mirror that reflected and parodied a brighter world of lovers whose reckless abandon to their cause is sane', but his own experience calls into question any so confident a separation of healthy from diseased.

Previous McEwan novels have contained genre elements ... and a few moments in the new novel demonstrate that he is not above raising the occasional goosebump ... But a story that begins with a set piece builds to no comparable climax ... It's disappointing that a book that begins so full-throatedly should end with stagy confrontation, then case history, references and appendices.

At one time, it would have seemed inconceivable for Ian McEwan to write a novel with a childless couple at its heart, so central did parenthood seem to his idea of human completeness. Clarissa is unable to conceive, and has adjusted to this condition with grace and warmth, by involving herself strongly with her many godchildren. Still, from time to time, 'the unconceived child' briefly stirs in her. The theme of parenting re-emerges near the end of the book, but Clarissa for all her grounded emotions and insights, has a lower status than, say, Julie in *The Child in Time*. McEwan's emotional engagement with feminism is less deferent than once it was.

Joe is a jack of all sciences, while Clarissa is an academic whose speciality is Keats. McEwan can't resist equipping Joe with a full expressive panoply of language. In theory, he and she occupy different worlds, in practice he inhabits both – one chapter is even done from his imagining her point of view, with Joe presented in the third person. Yet this imbalance is compensated for by the complexity of Joe's viewpoint, which embodies McEwan's fascination with science.

Joe reveres the hard science which once seemed his destined career, but can no longer aspire to it. His attempts to analyse behaviour without distortion are always being undone by needs he can't acknowledge, and he's at his most romantic when his language claims a scientific objectivity. Feeling a lurch of surprised love whenever he sees Clarissa after an absence, he tries to reconcile a unique pang with the big picture.

McEwan's last novel, *Black Dogs*, was oddly schematic, a lifeless conflict between reductive and open ways of looking at the world. *Enduring Love* is much the better book, despite its inability fully to dramatise its themes, perhaps because McEwan himself is richly divided between Joe's rationalism and something else.

When Joe rails against the poor science holdings of the London Library, and the assumption that the world is best understood through humanist culture, he forgets that his own livelihood as a populariser depends on there being a gap for him to bridge. So too the future of fiction is assured as long as direct self-knowledge is unattainable.

Adam Mars-Jones

Review 3 Blowing in the Wind

Ian McEwan's latest novel covers some of the territory familiar to his readers: obsession and its consequences, violent events, moral dilemmas. But *Enduring Love* also shows a new tenderness.

It begins like a movie, or a dream. Joe Rose has taken his wife Clarissa for a picnic in a Chilterns field. It is a lovers' reunion: she has been away for some weeks, doing research into some lost love letters of John Keats; he has lovingly bought an expensive birthday present and a nouveau Italian feast of mozzarella, focaccia and olives, and a 1987 Daumas Gassac. Meeting her at the airport, waiting at the arrivals gate in a crowd of eager others, Joe, a scientist, decides that Darwin was right about the universality of expressions of emotion in human beings: 'I saw the same joy, the same uncontrollable smile, in the faces of a Nigerian earth mother, a thin-lipped Scottish granny and a pale, correct Japanese businessman as they wheeled their trolleys in and recognised a figure in the expectant crowd.'

There is a great deal of love around in *Enduring Love*. From its first pages, McEwan stamps on to the narrative his double trademark: he creates an opening that is unforgettable (like that of *The Child in Time*), he leaves us in no doubt about his main theme, and at the same time wraps us up in so much movement that we have very little time to think about it.

For it's back to the action shots, to the Chilterns field and the Daumas Gassac.

The camera zooms in on the neck of the bottle, cool in its black foil; the soundtrack picks up random shouts, a child's cry, disjointed sounds carried on the wind. Change of camera-angle: from the eye of a buzzard wheeling overhead we see several tiny figures, men running from all corners of the field towards a hot-air balloon that is blowing and jumping out of control, a child frozen with terror inside the basket.

It all happens quickly, of course, and rather preposterously, as things do in life: the five converging men grab the dangling ropes, everything seems safe, then a small movement is bungled and a strong gust lifts the basket, suddenly the men are hanging above the ground. 'What is certain is that if we had not broken ranks, our collective weight would have brought the balloon to earth a quarter of the way down the slope a few seconds later as the gust subsided.' But 'letting go was in our nature, too' and so 'our crew enacted morality's ancient, irresolvable dilemma: us, or me'.

One man is carried off by the balloon, falls from a height and is killed. There is a brilliant and haunting description of his collapsed body sitting uncannily upright in the middle of a field, the bones internally shattered so that it was nothing but a loose and formless bag, 'a head on a thickened stick'. But McEwan does the same again – leaves us no time to absorb the shock, or to linger over the moral dilemmas he has outlined for us (whose fault was it? could they have prevented it? is self-preservation a stronger human urge than co-operation?). For, at the moment of this drama and this death, something else has happened, the thing that is to shape the rest of the novel and to play counterpoint to the theme he has already begun to weave.

What has happened is that Jed Parry, one of the other men brought there by chance, trying to save the balloon has taken one look at Joe Rose and fallen madly and obsessively in love with him. Parry is a young and skinny religious fanatic with high cheekbones, bright new trainers, a ponytail and (we later discover) a private income – all useful attributes, it turns out, for a successful stalker. And indeed he turns out to be the most determined and resourceful of stalkers, always there, (even in the London Library), always watching and writing and calling, constantly and unabashedly invoking God and the higher purpose. He also evolves a nightmarish twist to the basic business of obsession: Parry is convinced that it was Joe who fell in love with him, rather than the other way round ...

In the face of such craziness, what would you do? Laugh? Or somehow watch helplessly, as Joe does, while Parry's obsession slowly corrodes his confidence and his life, and inserts tiny levers into 'the fine crack of estrangement' that opens between him and Clarissa? McEwan's task here is a difficult one. He has created a powerfully real picture of a loving, even passionate marriage; a rounded and compelling character in Clarissa; in Joe a coolly intellectual (if intellectually disappointed) scientist who digresses on the topic of theories, like that of Einstein, which are accepted for reasons of their elegance. Now his authorial job is to make us believe that a nutcase like Parry, however insinuating, could destabilise this pair to the point where they separate. A theory surely rejected for reasons of inelegance.

There are subplots – the widow of the fallen man has to find out why he was in the field at all; Joe tries to revive his academic career. There is a moment of mistaken, murderous violence as the denouement comes: McEwan has a weakness for the rough stuff, and is very good at it, as he showed in *The Innocent*. There is also an overlay of science – now so fashionable in the literary novel (c.f. Jeanette Winterson and others) – which is put to use pointing up moral dilemmas, or thoughts on the human condition, and which we could probably manage without.

If the science is the novel's least convincing element then its core, the devastating effect of obsession on normality, the power of pathological love against the merely loving, is never in doubt. McEwan does a superb job of making us believe what seems so unlikely, and that is the book's great power. At the end come several appendices, mainly on De Clérambault's Syndrome (Parry's problem, since you ask). This is a mildly disappointing way to finish such a fine book (when does post-modern begin to look quaint?) and if I had been reading the novel purely for fun I would probably have skipped them. If I had, though, I would never have found out what happened to Clarissa and Joe, and their version of enduring love.

Jan Dalley

Reading the novel from critical positions

Some readers and critics deliberately choose to read from a particular critical position. They use this critical position to inform, extend or even take the place of their own individual, personal responses.

- Read each one carefully and talk about which aspects of the text each one is most interested in. Try and match each reading to the critical position it best describes. With which position do you have most sympathy?

Feminists:
- are interested in how women are represented in texts written by men
- explore the way these texts display the power relations between the sexes.

Structuralists and post-structuralists:
- are interested in the way language is used, not simply to describe the world, but to construct it
- are most interested in how the text is constructed: its form, its overall structure and the patterns of language in it, especially pairs of opposites
- are sometimes more interested in the gaps, silences and absences in texts.

Genre critics:
- believe that all literature can be classified into various types, or forms, such as tragedy, comedy, romance, thriller, epic, lyric and so on
- look for ways in which the text relates to the conventions of its genre
- argue that you can only really make sense of a text when you recognise the tradition to which it belongs.

Psychoanalytic critics:
- are interested in the unconscious
- pay most attention to what is glossed over or 'repressed'
- look beyond the obvious surface meaning to what the text is 'really' about
- look for representations of psychological states or phases in literature
- are more interested in the emotional conflicts between the characters than in the wider context.

Historical critics (Cultural materialists/Marxists):
- read historical and other relevant texts, alongside the literary ones, in order to see more clearly the context in which the literature was produced, and to recover its history
- read literature to understand the class struggle at various times and in various places, and to explore the causes of conflict between the privileged and the working class
- argue it is important to relate a text to the social context of its author and the historical contexts in which it was written and is read.

- Talk about the different insights each reading gives into *Enduring Love*. In what ways do the different readings help you to develop an informed response to the novel?

- Choose one of the readings and use it to help you write your own critical analysis of the novel.

Reading one

Enduring Love is preoccupied by the interests and concerns of the 1990s. As such it is a typical novel of the period. The contemporary details are spot on: from ciabatta bread, the bottle of Daumas-Gassac and the loft apartment, to the successful careers in the media and academia. Despite the repeated references to the key consumer items of the period, there is little sense of the world beyond the lives of this one couple. This emphasis on the personal world captures the self-obsessed quality of the 1990s society.

The ease with which Joe and Clarissa's secure middle class world is threatened and destabilised highlights the superficiality of late twentieth century success, revealing the anxieties and tensions lying beneath the veneer of complacency.

The different ways in which the characters try to make sense of these anxieties – science, religion, personal morality – is again typical of the middle class quest for a belief system which will give meaning to an increasingly materialistic world.

Reading two

Although the reader is encouraged to doubt the reliability of Joe, ultimately his rationalist view of the world is proved to be correct. Clarissa, in love with poetry and that most female friendly of poets, Keats, is shown to be sympathetic to psychotic love. Like Clarissa, Jean Logan – the only other female character – is revealed to be hopelessly mistaken in her interpretation of events, distracted from the truth by her emotional and hysterical reaction. In this novel emotion is associated with the irrational, the delusional and homosexual. Science, rationality, guns and the world of the thriller and detective novel belong to real men.

Clarissa is given very little space in the novel – just a chapter in which Joe imagines what she might have thought and a few scornfully dismissed extracts from a letter. This suggests that Joe's views are shared by his creator.

Reading three

Enduring Love exemplifies the post-modern novel. It begins by establishing a series of oppositions: rational/emotional; science/arts; sane/psychotic; male/female. Through the eyes of the narrator, Joe, the reader is encouraged to see the former in each pair as dominant. However, as the novel progresses, the oppositions seem less stable – can Joe's resolutely rational world make sense of a life which seems increasingly out of control? In the middle section of the novel, the reader's faith in Joe's reliability is stretched and we begin to think that the oppositions will be reversed and emotion will be shown to triumph.

Finally, although Joe is proved to be correct, we are left in no doubt that the oppositions are not as stable as they first appeared: his rational views have brought him dangerously close to the edge of sanity.

The repeated references to the act of interpretation, storytelling and the impossibility of objectivity; the confusion of genres and the refusal of the novel to end confirm this as a very 'post-modern' modern novel.

Reading four

Readers have frequently criticised the episode in *Enduring Love* where Joe goes to buy the gun as unrealistic, not fitting with the rest of the novel. Indeed, it does not 'fit' with the contemporary social drama or love story. It belongs to the genre of the thriller – the hero forced to go it alone, arriving back in the nick of time to rescue the damsel in distress. Despite its very modern feel – the contemporary setting, the discussion of scientific ideas and the concern with storytelling – recognising the features of the thriller in the novel gives the reader insight into just what a traditional tale this is.

Reading five

The fact that a psychological disorder is central to *Enduring Love* should not distract the reader from uncovering what this novel, like the main character, tries to repress.

In chapter 9, McEwan presents his first person narrator imagining the point of view of his female partner, showing some awareness of the contradictions in his own behaviour. This creates an expectation in the reader that Joe will continue to develop psychologically. This, however, is not the case and Joe becomes obsessed with proving that Jed's love for him is psychotic.

Joe's diagnosis of Jed's obsession as a symptom of de Clérambault's syndrome, and his ultimate vindication, shifts attention away from the true source of his anxieties: his fear of a homosexual relationship. His refusal to confide in Clarissa and his desire to retreat into the world of pure science suggest an even more profound inability to accept his emotional needs.

The move into the genre of the thriller further reveals the novel's repression of the conflict at its heart: between homosexual and heterosexual relationships. Joe's shooting of Jed and his successful rescue of Clarissa underline the character's and the novel's anxieties over sexuality.

A chapter by chapter summary of the novel

Chapter 1
Joe Rose's account of 'The beginning' of it all. Joe and Clarissa, re-united after a long separation, celebrate with a picnic in the Chiltern Hills. This is interrupted by the balloon accident which results in John Logan's death. Joe's interest in human behaviour is established – he analyses events in terms of evolutionary psychology, not just human emotions.

Chapter 2
Joe is aware of his role as storyteller as well as participant in events. The first encounter between Joe and Jed in the field beside the dead body of John Logan. Jed wants Joe to pray with him and Joe refuses. Dropping clues about the significance of events.

Chapter 3
The evening of the accident. Clarissa and Joe endlessly re-tell the story from their different points of view. Establishes the difference between Joe and Clarissa. In bed, Joe receives a phone call from Jed. He doesn't tell Clarissa about it.

Chapter 4
Return to their ordinary lives. Joe's disquiet that he is responsible for John Logan's death. Constant need to re-tell the story of the accident. Joe realises he is being followed.

Chapter 5
Connects the red and white trainer with Jed – first suggestion that he is being stalked. Digression on the difference between science and the arts. His own frustration with his job as a populariser of science. Rationalises his fear in terms of biology. Does not share his fears with Clarissa.

Chapter 6
Joe worrying away at who was responsible for Logan's death. Joe tells Clarissa about Jed – she is amused. Jed rings when Clarissa is out. Joe agrees to meet him 'just this once'.

Chapter 7
First meeting with Jed. No connection between their individual interpretations of their 'relationship'.

Chapter 8
Joe recalls discussions with Clarissa which highlight the different ways they make sense of the world. Clarissa objects to the reduction of everything to science. Jed keeps a vigil outside the house. When Joe refuses to talk to him, Jed begins ringing. Joe reports the 'stalking' to the police who can do nothing about it. Joe deletes all 29 of Jed's messages. Jed believes Joe is communicating with him via the curtains.

Chapter 9
Joe imagines what happens when Clarissa returns from work from her point of view. Told in the third person. Returning from work, she finds Joe in a manic and self-obsessed state. First argument in which Clarissa suggests that perhaps it is Joe who has a 'fixation' with Jed. Joe storms out. Jed is still waiting outside, out of sight of the house.

Chapter 10
First person, from Joe's point of view. Immediately after the argument. Jed chases him through the rainy streets. Thriller/detective genre. Joe thinks Jed's use of the word 'signal' is a clue.

Chapter 11
First letter from Jed provides another perspective. No commentary from Joe. His version of the story bears no relation to Joe's. Writes confidently about the love between Joe and himself and claims that Joe initiated the 'relationship'. Jed recounts 'how I live, where I live, my past, my story'.

Chapter 12
Joe's visit to John Logan's wife, Jean. While travelling there, he recounts Clarissa's reactions to Jed, her scepticism and the rift growing between them. Has persuaded himself that perhaps it

is Clarissa who is having an affair and goes through the letters in her study. Interprets his own behaviour in the context of evolutionary psychology and self persuasion.

Chapter 13
Meets Jean Logan. She has her own explanation for why John died.

Chapter 14
Joe with the Logan children. Jean interprets the open car doors as evidence that John was having an affair. She wants Joe to help her find the woman and ask the others about their memories of the car door. A chance remark from Leo helps Joe identify the illness from which he is sure Jed is suffering – de Clérambault's syndrome.

Chapter 15
Returns from Oxford. Joe thinks about de Clérambault's syndrome and its connection with love. Jed is waiting for him. There is a change in him – a 'hardness' and an implicit threat of violence. Clarissa has discovered his intrusion into her study. She interprets the open drawer as a signal which she is unable to interpret.

Chapter 16
Second letter from Jed. Critical analysis of Joe's atheistic and scientific explanation of the world.

Chapter 17
Joe's research confirms that sufferers of de Clérambault's syndrome often turn violent. Joe and Clarissa's relationship deteriorating. Clarissa thinks Joe needs help.

Chapter 18
Clarissa's birthday. Pretence that everything between them is fine. Joe visits the police station. His fears are not taken seriously.

Chapter 19
Originally the opening chapter. Clarissa's birthday meal in the restaurant. A gunman shoots the man at the next table. Joe is convinced it was meant for him.

Chapter 20
Joe can't get the police to believe the bullet was meant for him. Discussion of memory and unreliability of stories. Contacts Johnny B to get hold of a gun.

Chapter 21
Thriller conventions. Visiting the hippy household to get the gun. Clarissa calls his mobile; she is being held by Jed.

Chapter 22
Joe practises shooting the gun. Even as he is panicking, he is thinking scientifically, placing human behaviour in the context of biology. At the apartment, we hear Jed's story. Joe shoots Jed to stop him slitting his own throat. Move from action to reflection and commentary on the other ways in which the story could have developed, but didn't.

Chapter 23
Clarissa has moved out. Letter telling the story from her point of view. Joe's reaction to this.

Chapter 24
Concludes the sub-plot with the Logans. Hints of a reconciliation between Joe and Clarissa.

Appendix 1
An invented discussion of de Clérambault's syndrome and an invented case study based on McEwan's story. Lets us know that Clarissa and Joe got back together.

Appendix 2
Letter from Jed.

Teachers' notes

The interview

Students might find it helpful to watch the interview with Ian McEwan soon after their first, individual reading of the novels, before going on to study it in more detail.

If you are reading the novel together in sections, incorporating activities into the first reading, 'A suggested route through the novel' suggests suitable points at which to view and discuss the different sections of the interview. Students could then watch the whole interview, using the questions on pages 37 and 38 to help them consolidate their thinking.

A first reading

This is a challenging novel for students, raising difficult philosophical and moral ideas. However, it is also a gripping and dramatic page turner. As students read it for the first time, they might find it helpful to use post-it notes to identify sections which they find difficult or where they feel lost. These could either be explored in the subsequent lesson or put to one side and returned to after the first reading. It is helpful if all students have some knowledge of the basic story and events early on in their study of it so that key aspects can be discussed in the context of the whole novel.

Using the summary

Consolidate students' individual reading by using the summary in the pack. You could:

– get students to read the summary for the chapters they have just read and consider whether they would add anything else

– use it to consider what the focus is at this point in the novel (for example, the relationship between Clarissa and Joe; Joe's career; Joe's anxiety about Jed; the ballooning accident or its aftermath)

– ask students to write their own summary of the chapters they have just read and compare it with the one in the pack

– write summaries from the point of view of different characters in the novel (for example, what does Clarissa think has been happening during this time?). Ask students to think about what gave them their ideas.

Key quotations

For each chapter, individuals could pick out short quotations that seem to be key to the ideas or characters in that chapter. Before going onto the next chunk of reading, share these in small groups. Compare choices and talk about the significance of each.

A suggested route through the novel and the material in the pack

If the students have not read or listened to the whole novel, and you are using the pack to support students *during* reading, you will need to miss out or adapt short sections of the activities in order to keep the ending, including the appendices, a surprise.

Possible stopping points: end of chapters 1, 5, 9, 18, 21, the end.

Before reading

● Introductory activity: the conversation on page 32.

Beginning reading – chapter 1

● Detailed work on the opening: first responses to the character of Joe, the style and the point of view.

● Listen to the interview on the opening (sections 2-4); compare what McEwan says about the character of Joe and so on, with own ideas. Use to establish the type of novel it is; the characters; initial relationships; the dilemma.

● Students' own writing: a synopsis for the novel – what do you think will happen? An alternative would be to do this as an oral activity.

● To give students the chance to sort out what actually happens in chapter 1, ask the class, either individually or in pairs, to write the newspaper report of the balloon accident. The aim should be to make this as objective a report as possible.

Chapters 2-5

- Continue reading to chapter 5. Summarise the novel so far and compare with the summary provided in the pack.
- Video extract 3: establishing the character of Joe.
- Introducing the characters in role. See the activity on pages 45-46.
- Begin tracing response to characters (see the activity on page 45.) Alternatively, wait until chapter 9 and use this activity as an opportunity to recap.
- Look back at chapters 1-4 and complete the activities on page 47: 'Characters' stories and interpretations'.
- Use work on genre on page 39 of the pack to explore the use of different genres to shape the response of the reader, particularly in chapters 3 and 5. Watch video extract 5: 'Playing with genre'.
- Have a go at writing about a short incident, for example an argument, in a 'stream of consciousness' style, tracking thoughts, emotions, interpretations of what is said and so on. Compare this with the way McEwan conveys the minute by minute shifts in Joe's thinking and emotional responses.
- Begin to draw up a chart for the novel comparing chronological time and narrative time (see page 44). Use this to focus discussion on the ways in which McEwan tells the story.
- Use chapter 5 to think about the role of science in the novel. Use the following activities: 'Science in the novel' (page 51) and 'The Science/Arts divide' (on page 62). Watch video extract 10.

Reading chapters 5-9

- Prepare dramatic readings of chapters 6, 7, 8 with different students taking on the role of the main characters and reading the dialogue. Focus discussion on: the way the story is told, including point of view and the way McEwan presents the characters. Continue to trace response to the characters.
- Read up to the beginning of chapter 9 (Clarissa's point of view). Summarise the events so far from the points of view of Joe, Clarissa and Jed. Compare these.
- Activities on point of view (page 48 of the pack), including the letters. Look back at either chapter 3 or 5 and have a go at writing a letter or diary in role as either Jed or Clarissa.
- Continue tracing responses to the characters.
- The character of Joe and the unreliable narrator. Use interview extract 6.

Reading chapters 10 – 18

- Watch video extract 8: 'Love' and talk about the significance of the title.

Reading chapters 19, 20 and 21

- Read and discuss the restaurant scene and the police station scene. Recap work on point of view, reliability of Joe and the presentation of characters.
- Read up to the end of the gun scene, and recap the work on genre.
- Read up to the end of Chapter 21. Predict or write the end of the novel.

Reading chapters 22, 23, 24 and the appendices

- Finish reading the novel. Conclude work on tracing responses to the characters.

- Read the appendices of the novel, recording responses to each one. Talk about how the appendices successively modify your response to the novel as a whole.
- Do the work on the appendices on page 58.

After reading

- Watch the whole interview, and use the guiding questions on pages 37-38 to consolidate work on the novel.
- Interpretations by other readers (page 65).

Notes on 'A conversation' (page 32)
Provide students with the following contextual material about the conversation a piece at a time.

- It is a conversation between two men.
- They have met only once before.
- One of the men is married.
- One of the men is a science writer.
- The novel is written by a man.
- The writer is famous for writing macabre fiction.
- The novel from which the conversation is taken was critically acclaimed and is a best-seller.

Regeneration

by

Pat Barker

Exploring the contexts of the novel

First thoughts about the First World War

As a reader of *Regeneration*, early in the twenty-first century, you will undoubtedly come to it with all kinds of ideas about the First World War. Before you start studying the novel, it is worth spending a short time analysing what those ideas are and where they come from.

- On your own, select from this list of words and phrases the ones that seem to you to be most appropriate to the First World War.

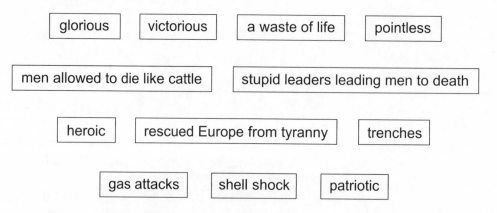

| glorious | victorious | a waste of life | pointless |

| men allowed to die like cattle | stupid leaders leading men to death |

| heroic | rescued Europe from tyranny | trenches |

| gas attacks | shell shock | patriotic |

- Where do you think your view of the War comes from:
  - novels
  - film/TV images
  - photographs
  - poetry
  - family history
  - history books/history lessons?

- Pool your ideas in small groups, keeping a note of your thoughts, to look back at after you have read the novel and discovered more about the world it portrays.

Reading the first chapter – considering contexts

- On your own, read the first chapter and talk about your first responses, in terms of:
  - pleasure
  - interest
  - high and low points
  - expectations of the rest of the novel.

- How much do you think you will need to know about the different contexts of the novel, firstly in order to enjoy it and secondly, in order to interpret and write critically about it? To what extent might the novel provide its own contextual background?

- Look again in more detail at the first chapter. Talk about it and, either annotate it or take notes to show what contexts you think you may need to be aware of, or have knowledge of, to develop an informed reading. You may want to think about historical, cultural, literary and linguistic contexts relating to:

- the period Pat Barker is writing about (the First World War), for example did Sassoon really write the Declaration?
- the period when she was writing the novel (the late twentieth century).

● Share your ideas and decide which contexts seem most important and useful to consider and which are only of marginal use.

Myth or truth – reading and interpreting the First World War

● Look back at your first ideas about the First World War, collected before you read any of the novel. Talk briefly about how your ideas have been confirmed or challenged by reading the first chapter.

● Look at the two extracts on pages 78-79 from books about the First World War and its impact on us now.

● In small groups talk about:
   - what view of the war each takes and whether there is anything that changes or challenges your previous ideas
   - what the extracts suggest about the differences between attitudes before the war and since the war
   - what the extracts suggest about the way the war has been 'mythologised' by subsequent generations
   - whether, and in what ways reading these texts alters your ideas about the First World War
   - whether, and in what ways reading these texts alters your reading of the first chapter.

● Now read the letter from a soldier to his sisters on pages 80-81 and look at the photos on pages 82 and 83. Talk about the issues listed above in relation to these items.

● Finally, look at the extract from the opening of the film of Regeneration and talk again about the issues listed above. (Video clip timing: 00:32:09)

The Great War and Modern Memory

'At an inquest on the body of Arthur Sydney Evelyn Annesley, aged 49, formerly a captain in the Rifle Brigade, who committed suicide by flinging himself under a heavy van at Pimlico, the Coroner stated that worry caused by the feeling that he was not going to be accepted for service led him to take his life.' *The Times*, August 9, 1914.

... the Great War was perhaps the last to be conceived as taking place within a seamless, purposeful 'history' involving a coherent stream of time running from past through present to future. The shrewd recruiting poster depicting a worried father of the future being asked by his children, 'Daddy, what did *you* do in the Great War?' assumes a future whose moral and social pressures are identical with those of the past. Today, when each day's experience seems notably *ad hoc*, no such appeal would shame the most stupid to the recruiting office. But the Great War took place in what was, compared with ours, a static world, where the values appeared stable and where the meanings of abstractions seemed permanent and reliable. Everyone knew what Glory was, and what Honour meant. It was not until eleven years after the war that Hemingway could declare in *A Farewell to Arms* that 'abstract words such as glory, honour, courage or hallow were obscene beside the concrete names of villages, the number of roads, the names of rivers, the numbers of regiments and the dates'. In the summer of 1914 no one would have understood what on earth he was talking about.

Certainly the author of a personal communication in *The Times* two days before the declaration of war would not have understood:

'PAULINE – Alas, it cannot be. But I will dash into the great venture with all that pride and spirit an ancient race has given me...'

The language is that which two generations of readers had been accustomed to associate with the quiet action of personal control and Christian self-abnegation ('sacrifice'), as well as with more violent actions of aggression and defense. The tutors in this special diction had been the boys' books of George Alfred Henty; the male-romances of Rider Haggard; the poems of Robert Bridges; and especially the Arthurian poems of Tennyson and the pseudo-medieval romances of William Morris.

... a striking phenomenon of the last twenty-five years is this obsession with the images and myths of the Great War among novelists and poets too young to have experienced it directly. They have worked it up by purely literary means, means which necessarily transform the war into a 'subject' and simplify its motifs into myths and figures expressive of the modern existential predicament. These writers provide for the 'post-modern' sensibility a telling example of the way the present influences the past. In eschewing the Second World War as a source of myth and instead jumping back to its predecessor, these writers have derived their myth in the way Frye notes most critics derive their principles, not from their predecessors but from their predecessors' predecessors.

Paul Fussell

The First World War

… It has, as the war recedes into history, become fashionable to decry the lament for a 'Lost Generation' as myth-making. The loss, demographers demonstrate, was swiftly made good by natural increase of population, while loss was felt, the harder-hearted sort of historian insists, by a fraction of families. At the very worst, they argue, only 20 per cent of those who went to the war did not return, while the aggregate was lower, 10 per cent or less. For the majority, the war was but a passage in their lives, an interruption of normality to which society rapidly returned as soon as the guns fell silent.

This is a complacent judgement. It is true that the Great War, by comparison with that of 1939-45, did little material damage. No large European city was destroyed or even seriously devastated during its course, as all large German cities were by aerial bombardment during the Second World War. The First World War was a rural conflict on the Eastern as on the Western Fronts. The fields over which it was fought were swiftly returned to agriculture or pasturage and the villages ruined by bombardment – except for those around Verdun – quickly rebuilt. The war inflicted no harm to Europe's cultural heritage that was not easily repaired: the medieval Cloth Hall at Ypres stands today as it did before the bombardments of 1914-18, so do the town squares of Arras, so does the cathedral of Rouen, while the treasures of Louvain, burnt in an uncharacteristic act of vandalism in 1914, were replaced piece by piece in the war's aftermath.

Above all, the war imposed on the civilian populations involved almost none of the deliberate disruption and atrocity that was to be a feature of the Second. Except in Serbia and, at the outset, in Belgium, communities were not forced to leave their homes, land and peaceful occupations; except in Turkish Armenia, no population was subjected to genocide; and, awful though the Ottoman government's treatment of its Armenian subjects was, the forced march organised to do them to death belongs more properly to the history of Ottoman imperial policy than to that of the war itself. The First, unlike the Second World War, saw no systematic displacement of populations, no deliberate starvation, no expropriation, little massacre or atrocity. It was, despite the efforts by state propaganda machines to prove otherwise, and the cruelties of the battlefield apart, a curiously civilised war.

Yet it damaged civilisation, the rational and liberal civilisation of the European enlightenment, permanently for the worse and, through the damage done, world civilisation also. …

In 1939 the apprehension of war was strong, so was its menace, so, too, was knowledge of its reality. In 1914, by contrast, war came, out of a cloudless sky, to populations which knew almost nothing of it and had been raised to doubt that it could ever again trouble their continent.

John Keegan

A letter from a wounded soldier to his sisters

Ashbourne Red Cross Hospital
15th May, 1917

My Dear Sisters

In the first place I never wrote you from France, as I could say very little owing to the strict censorship, and out there letter writing was not easy owing to the cold and wet, and few facilities for writing, and again whenever I got the chance I always wrote Jenny…

I left Arras on Sunday 18th March at 10.30 at night after having been on three working parties that day, and was more dead than alive when I arrived at billets about 1a.m. The marching with full pack is very hard work. Next day we marched to Izel-ler-Ham …for training preparatory for the great Advance. I knew it was coming off, and I wanted very much to warn Finlay in case I got 'Na pooked,' as we say, but I could not find a way. However back we went to Arras on Monday 2nd April. It was a very trying march up, owing to snow and a good bit of the way being like a pond. We had to march about 14 miles with only one fall out for ten minutes. About this time I was appointed officers' mess waiter on account of it being lighter work, so I did not need to do any working parties, but I spent the few days before the 9th in a dug out.

Well the 9th of April came round, and I went into the front line about 2a.m. The hours wore round until 5a.m. 5.30 was the hour to go 'Over the top'. At 5a.m. word was passed along 'Half an hour to go, boys.' At 5.25, 'Five minutes to go, Boys', and then at 5.30 sharp a mine exploded on our left as a signal, and over we went. Before that hour there was no sign of life, and only the usual artillery fire going on. On the signal being given, in half a minute the ground was swarming with men with fixed bayonets, and the barrage started. I can hardly describe my feelings on paper, but all I can say is, it *was* exciting. The artillery fire was indescribable. A bombardment like it had never been heard. The Germans were completely surprised. A good number of prisoners were taken in a short time. The objective of our company ('A') was 'Fred's Wood', and we got there with very little loss, and dug ourselves in beyond the Wood.

During the forenoon we had to stand a good bit of shelling, and an old school mate of Tom's in my company was killed then. During the forenoon it was a wonderful sight to see the troops to right and left of us (we could see a considerable distance) moving forward, and the shell barrage bursting a short distance in front of them. We moved up the line of advance in the afternoon, and were put into a shallow trench for the night to make the best of it. We dug ourselves down five or six feet, but it was impossible to sleep. We had snow, rain and hail in turns a good part of the night, and only a waterproof sheet to cover us. In the middle of the night I was called out, and had to go about $1^1/_2$ miles over very rough ground, and bring back water for the company. When daylight came we went across to a battered village and got some firewood, and so we were able to make tea and cocoa. In the afternoon we were taken further on, and halted on a railway embankment where we lay 2 or 3 hours. The snow came down and covered us, but we could not move. Shells were dropping on the opposite bank, and we could not go on the rails, as Fritz had a machine gun trained on them. We were then taken back a bit, and put into a stable in what was left of a village; I think Fenchy was the name of it. I lay down just as I was and slept an hour or two, when I was called about 10.30p.m. to go on a ration party. On returning, the rations were served out, and we were able to get a meal, tea, bully and biscuits. I lay down again about 12, and fell asleep, and was wakened again at 2, and the order was, 'Fall in at the double,' that is, in a hurry. We were then marched away up the line, ignorant of our destination. We were taken across a plain intersected by trenches in which were a lot of our troops. Then our Colonel stopped us, and speaking quietly, told us to uphold the name of the R.S.F. as being second to none. That was the first intimation that we were going into action. We then formed up for attack in line with the other regiments of our brigade, the 45th, and advanced. In a few minutes we came to a low bank. It was growing light at this time. On getting over this bank Fritz spotted us, and then the band played. We had no artillery support this time, as our guns were not up. Fritz, on seeing us opened fire with machine guns and rifles. The racket they made was awful, the bullets were flying everywhere. I could see the snow being flicked up by them hitting the ground. Men began to fall right and left. It was pandemonium. Fritz then sent up rockets as signals to his artillery, and shells began to fall. Still our men went on. In my case I kept well in the front. I got to a trench and rested a little, then into another where I managed to get potting at Fritz. I got some of my own back here. I had just one field to cross to Fritz's front line. I got up again, and was within about 30 yards of Fritz's trench, when a bullet went through my thigh, and smashed my water bottle. I had to give up then as I could not walk. It is a marvel to me how any man could go through that fire, and not get hit, yet many did, but alas, many did not, and many fell never to rise again. I will never forget that morning as long as I live. I managed then to crawl to the rear where I got my field-dressing put on, and then got assistance back to the dressing station. I then was carried on a stretched back to Arras, a distance of about five miles over rough country. I was knocked out at the taking of Monchy-le-Preux. From Arras I was taken by motor to a clearing station, and put into a train, where I got the first meal I had had for 24 hours, except for a mouthful of biscuit, and a few drinks of tea. I was taken to Boulogne base hospital, where I lay 13 days. Then I was sent to Blighty, and arrived in Derby. I was in the Infirmary there for 13 days, when I was sent to where I am now. I cannot speak too highly of the attention and kindness shown to patients in any hospital I have been in. Where I am at present is a good convalescent home. It is a small town, and the countryside round about is very nice. I have been away in the Doctor's motor for a run twice. I am getting on very well and my wound is almost healed up now. I suffered more from rheumatism than I did from the wound. I must consider myself lucky getting a bullet flesh wound. Some of the men got terribly smashed...

I remain,
Your affec. brother,
Jack.

Jack Robertson (bottom left) went back to the Front only to be killed at Ypres.

Photographs of the First World War

Photographs of the First World War

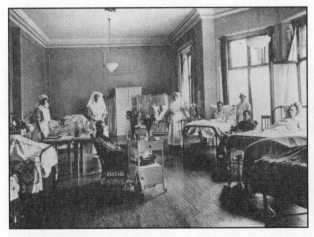

A Soldier's Declaration

- Now that you have looked at a few texts exploring the period in which the novel is set, re-read Sassoon's 'A Soldier's Declaration' on the first page of the novel. Try reading it from the point of view of:
  - a General, responsible for trying to bring the war to a victorious end
  - a member of Sassoon's close family
  - a conscientious objector
  - Jack, the writer of the letter to his sisters
  - yourself, as a 21st century reader.

- Share your ideas about their possible responses, taking into account the attitudes to war, the likely mood in the country at the time and the attitudes towards the war today.

Two poems by Sassoon

- In small groups, read one of these poems Siegfried Sassoon, one of the 'real people' who appears as a character in *Regeneration*.

Banishment

I am banished from the patient men who fight
They smote my heart to pity, built my pride.
Shoulder to aching shoulder, side by side,
They trudged away from life's broad wealds
                                    of light.
Their wrongs were mine; and ever in my sight
They went arrayed in honour. But they died,–
Not one by one; and mutinous I cried
To those who sent them out into the night.

The darkness tells how vainly I have striven
To free them from the pit where they must dwell
In outcast gloom convulsed and jagged and riven
By grappling guns. Love drove me to rebel.
Love drives me back to grope with them
                                    through hell;
And in their tortured eyes I stand forgiven.
                        (Craiglockhart, 1917)

Survivors

No doubt they'll soon get well; the shock and strain
    Have caused their stammering,
                                    disconnected talk.
Of course they're 'longing to go out again,'–
    These boys with old, scared faces, learning
                                    to walk.
They'll soon forget their haunted nights; their
                                    cowed
    Subjection to the ghosts of friends who died, –
Their dreams that drip with murder; and
                                    they'll be proud
    Of glorious war that shatter'd all their pride...
Men who went out to battle, grim and glad;
Children, with eyes that hate you, broken and
                                    mad.
                    (Craiglockhart, October 1917)

- First talk about your group's poem in its own right, for example: what you find interesting about it; what you think it's about; what strikes you about its viewpoint, style and the language it uses to convey ideas and emotions.

- Next, talk about the poem in relation to the first chapter of the novel. What ideas does it give you about the world of the novel. You should think about:
  - the war and the trenches
  - the attitudes to the war at the time
  - the views of the writer.

- What insights does it give you into Sassoon as he appears as a character in the first chapter?

- Present your ideas about the poem to the rest of the group.

Consolidating your ideas about contexts

- Talk about the kinds of contexts you have explored in this section. In what ways, if at all, has this contextual information altered your response to Chapter 1 and shaped your expectations of the novel?

Reading the novel

Strategies for reading the novel

- Before you read *Regeneration*, you might find it helpful to complete 'A personal reading profile' in section 1 and talk about strategies for reading a novel.

- As you read the novel for the first time on your own, don't worry too much about anything you find puzzling. Use post-it notes to jot down questions or ideas and to identify any sections you would like to talk about in class.

- You could pause during the reading at key stages, such as the end of each part of the novel, in order to share your first responses.

Interview with Pat Barker

Using the interview

You might find it helpful to watch the interview with Pat Barker soon after your first reading of *Regeneration*, before going on to look more closely at key aspects of the novel.

- Pause at the end of each section of the interview and talk about the questions raised below.

1. The idea of the novel (00:33:17)
- Talk about any insights the interview gives you into the decision to focus the novel on Rivers and Craiglockhart.

2. The title (00:35:42)
- Compare the working title *On the Edge* with the title *Regeneration*. What does the interview contribute to your understanding of the importance of the metaphor of regeneration in the novel?

3. Rivers (00:37:03)
- Pat Barker focuses on the shape of the relationship between Rivers and Sassoon as being central to the novel. In what ways does this correspond with your first reading of the novel? Barker talks about the 'historical' Rivers. In what ways does her description give you insight into Rivers the character?

4. A perspective on the First World War (00:41:20)
- Look back at the section on page 83, which Barker refers to in the interview. Talk about what Owen says and the light Barker throws on this.

5. Fact and fiction (00:42:51)
- Think about what Barker says about putting a historical character against the background of a fictional character, to throw him into sharper relief. Talk about specific examples of how this works in the novel.
  What do you find interesting about what Barker says specifically about Prior?

6. Prior, Owen and the minor characters (00:45:58)

- Make a quick diagram, showing the key ideas Barker conveys about the different functions of the minor characters.

7. Exploring notions of masculinity (00:48:32)

- Use these headings as the starting-point for discussion: passivity and masculinity; relationships at the Front; breakdown and hysteria.

8. The women in the novel (00:53:44)

- What does the contextual information provided by Barker contribute to your understanding of the themes and characters?

9. Owen and Sassoon: the poetry (00:55:42)

- Is there anything surprising about Barker's account of the role Owen plays in the novel? Talk about what Barker is trying to say about the process of writing at the end of the section, when she talks about 'Russian dolls'.

10. Language and protest (00:58:36)

- Thinking about the novel as a whole, discuss the issues raised by Pat Barker, about silence, speech and protest.

11. Narrative voice and style (00:59:42)

- Think about what Barker has to say about the 'kind of drama within the therapeutic conversation'. Talk about whether you agree with her.
  Talk about her idea that 'less is more'. Is this how you see her presentation of the horror of the war, in *Regeneration*?

12. First World War fictions at the end of the twentieth century (1:03:16)

- Explore what you think Barker is saying about the reasons for our particular interest in the First World War at this stage in history and whether you agree with her analysis.

13. The novel and the film (1:04:45)

- Talk about Barker's view of what film can and cannot do, as compared with fiction. If you have an opportunity to see the film, think again about what she says and consider whether you agree with her.

Exploring character

Characters and oppositions

- Think about these oppositions in the novel:

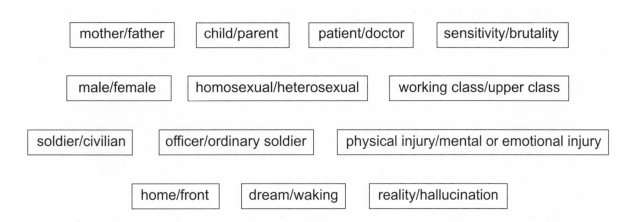

mother/father	child/parent	patient/doctor	sensitivity/brutality

male/female	homosexual/heterosexual	working class/upper class

soldier/civilian	officer/ordinary soldier	physical injury/mental or emotional injury

home/front	dream/waking	reality/hallucination

- In pairs, take responsibility for one of these oppositions. Write it in the centre of a blank piece of paper. Explore the opposition in terms of the characters in the novel by trying to place them on either side of the opposition and noting down comments as you go. How easy is it to do this?

An example is started for you below:

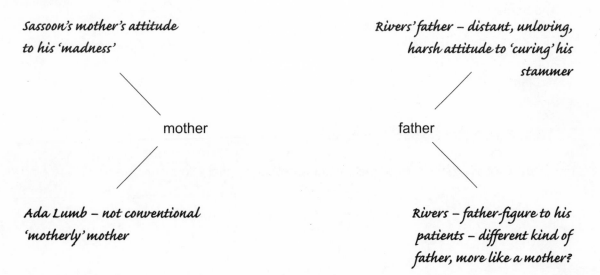

Sassoon's mother's attitude to his 'madness'

Rivers' father – distant, unloving, harsh attitude to 'curing' his stammer

mother

father

Ada Lumb – not conventional 'motherly' mother

Rivers – father-figure to his patients – different kind of father, more like a mother?

- Find a few quotations that seem particularly apt for that opposition and the characters you have grouped around it. For instance, if you are talking about the 'working class/upper class' opposition, you might want to quote Prior saying, 'You mustn't make too much of it, you know, the snobbery. I didn't. The only thing that really makes me angry is when people at home say there are no class distinctions at the front. Ball-*ocks*.' (Page 67)
  Write your quotations on your sheet of paper, in appropriate places.

- Present your ideas to the whole group, using your annotations to help you. After the session, you could display your annotations, or photocopy them for the group.

- In the period before the First World War, many of these oppositions were seen as quite separate and stable. For instance, the majority of people saw male and female qualities as opposites and as entirely fixed. What does the exploration of the oppositions in terms of characters in the novel reveal to you about the stability of these categories in the novel? What does the novel seem to be saying about the changes that occurred during the First World War?

Writing about characters and oppositions

- Choose one or two of the oppositions that interest you most and write a detailed exploration of the role of different characters in developing ideas about them.

The function of characters

- Look at this list of some of the main characters in the novel. Try to group them in terms of their function in the novel, for instance characters who challenge accepted ideas, characters who show the role of women at the time and so on. (A single character might fit into more than one of your groupings.)

  Rivers
  Burns
  Sassoon
  Graves
  Prior
  Owen
  Sarah Lumb
  Ada Lumb
  Anderson
  Willard
  Henry Head
  Ruth Head
  Yealland
  Bryce
  Brock
  The nurses: Sister Rogers, Matron etc.

- Talk about what difference it would make if any one of these characters were missing from the novel.

The character of Rivers

Finding an angle

Pat Barker, in her video interview, says that Rivers gave her the 'angle' she needed on the First World War.

> Discovering Rivers and Craiglockhart, and that whole story, was what finally managed to convince me that I could write something slightly different. I was very anxious not to do what I'm afraid I call a pseudo combatant book, where you absorb all the raw materials, which you can do very easily, you just soak yourself in it, and then you write about the trenches as if you'd been there. I was determined I wasn't going to do that. I wanted the central character, the central stand point to be that of somebody who hadn't fought, who knew a lot about it, who heard a lot about it, but, in the end, had not been there. And I got that in the figure of William Rivers, who was the psychiatrist at Craiglockhart.

- Read this piece by a pyschoanalyst, David Morgan, on Rivers and the history of psychoanalysis.

- In pairs or small groups, use highlighting and annotation to draw out what is most useful to you in developing your understanding of the historical figure of Rivers, whom Barker turns into her fictional character.

Rivers and the history of psychoanalysis

Pat Barker vividly depicts a particular time in the history of the western world, when many assumptions about human beings – what it meant to be male and female, the apparent differences between classes, the doctor-patient relationship and the whole idea of a benevolent authority where it was accepted that those in charge knew what they were doing – were thrown into crisis by the horror of the reality of a war that led to meaningless deaths. It was a loss of innocence. The old accepted ways were challenged because they failed to prevent such a terrible thing occurring.

This devastation of a generation of men and the emotional scarring of the families and loved ones they left behind, forced into consciousness an awareness of the sheer horror of what man can do to other men. As a result, there was a profound change in the way people thought about themselves and each other. This powerful change is illustrated in the novel by the relationship between Dr. Rivers and his damaged patients.

Psychoanalysis was in its infancy during the years of the First World War. Its most famous practitioner and discoverer was Sigmund Freud. The most important aspect of his theory was that mankind was motivated by powerful instinctive forces such as love and hate. Depending on what experiences an individual had, these forces were either mitigated by human involvement or they were not. This tended to make the individual more or less motivated by creativity or destructiveness. An important factor in this development was the capacity for insight into one's actions, feelings and thoughts. A way of helping people understand themselves was for psychoanalysts and psychotherapists to see their patients on an individual basis and encourage them to talk about themselves, their dreams and thoughts and experiences. This would allow the psychoanalyst to get to know the patient, particularly those parts that might have been repressed i.e. not consciously available in the patient's thoughts. Dr. Rivers was working with his shellshock victims and neurasthenic* patients before psychoanalysis had really developed as a method.

What Barker presents so accurately is a picture of a physician who despite his military training really cares about his patients. Unlike Dr. Yealland who performs electric shock therapy on his patients, or the less sensitive forms of treatment of other colleagues, Rivers gets to know his patients and what makes them tick, using early psychoanalytic ideas such as listening to and interpreting material according to the patient's experience of the past or present. In one case he also uses hypnotism* in the way that Freud also experimented with before he developed psychoanalysis. Here we have a humane man working in very difficult circumstances; he is an anthropologist as a well a doctor, he is interested in the meaning of things and not just in patching people up.

These days we have a deeper understanding of the effects of trauma on the individual mind. Rivers' patients would have been diagnosed as having post-traumatic stress disorder (PTSD) a label given to patients who present mental and physical symptoms triggered by some real life trauma to themselves or others. Like the people involved in the football tragedy at Hillsborough stadium, or refugees from Bosnia or soldiers on both sides of the Desert Storm war against Sadam Hussein and Iraq. These symptoms can seem unrelated to the actual original trauma and can occur as avoidance, panic attacks, hallucinations, mutism (not speaking), paralysis (being unable to move) or even anorexia. It was Freud's view, mirrored by Rivers in his sensitive treatment of his patients, that you could help a patient's symptoms by uncovering the patient's fears that have been repressed or pushed to the back of the mind where they become unconscious. In this unconscious state the fears and anxieties associated with frightening events or experiences continue to influence the person's life and actions, almost unknown to him.

Human beings' minds and bodies are designed to avoid pain, both in physical and psychological terms. The body and mind are designed to recover from trauma as quickly as possible, so just as physical traumas of accidents and hospital operations are quickly forgotten once healing has occurred, so psychological traumas are repressed in the aid of getting a person back to 'normal'. This latter repression is probably a necessary defence – without it we would not be able to function. For instance we can hear about horrors on the T.V., and the next moment go and have our tea. Hopefully it doesn't mean that we don't care, but it is our capacity for splitting off from information that is too painful that allows us to carry on with our own lives. However, for those involved in the conflict of war, famine or any other physical and psychological trauma, such as a serious accident or the loss of a loved one, this capacity to withdraw from the painful experience is limited by the powerful force of having been exposed to something that remains unrepressable. It is helpful at these times to talk to someone like a psychoanalyst or similar professional who can understand what the underlying fears might be. This should only be explored within the context of a secure relationship. Rivers provides this secure relationship, he becomes a parental figure to the men, and encourages them to talk about themselves in a way none of them have done before.

This novel is set a long time before trauma was recognised as a response to great suffering. Indeed to be vulnerable in those times, particularly if you were a man, was considered in a very negative light.

*Neurasthenia is a psychiatric term used to denote psychological symptoms that express themselves in physical manifestations such as paralysis, mutism and panic attacks.

*Hypnosis or hypnotism is a technique designed to send the patient into a trance like state, by-passing consciousness to release repressed material. Freud largely became disillusioned with hypnosis because although it helped some patients retrieve memories, they largely forgot them again when they came out of the hypnotic state i.e. repression cannot really be by-passed. In this way, the fact that Rivers' hypnotism of Prior allows him to rediscover the lost traumatic memory, is a bit unrealistic.

The way Rivers changes and develops in the novel

Pat Barker, in her video interview says of Rivers:

> Rivers changes almost as much, if not more, than his patients. And this is one of the things that fascinated me, the idea, which Rivers himself as the historical figure was quite aware of, that as he changed his patients, his patients were also changing him. All the obituaries of Rivers refer to the fact that that single year at Craiglockhart transformed his personality completely. And at an age, in his early fifties, when people are popularly supposed to be incapable of radical change. But he certainly wasn't.
>
> One of the obituaries says that he cured himself in order to be able to cure others, and I think that's true. He was a paralytically shy man, because he had this dreadful stammer, he was over cautious, he was inhibited, he was a typical bachelor don, with very, very repressed emotions, very much the stiff upper lip, public school Englishman. And the only way he could reach out to these young men who were so traumatised was to stop being like that, and so he stopped. And, incidentally, not everybody thought it was an improvement, because he also became very bolshy and outspoken after the war, and some people preferred the old Rivers, who didn't make any waves.

● Look at these 5 extracts from the novel, showing Rivers at different moments. Talk about what view of him you gain. Look back at Pat Barker's comments and think about the extracts in the light of what she says.

1   Rivers hesitated. 'Look, I think we've ... we've got about as far as we can get today. You must be very tired.' He stood up. 'I'll see you tomorrow morning at ten. Oh, and could you ask Captain Graves to see me as soon as he arrives?'

Sassoon stood up. 'You said a bit back you didn't think I was mad.'

'I'm quite sure you're not. As a matter of fact I don't even think you've got a war neurosis.'

Sassoon digested this. 'What have I got, then?'

'You seem to have a very powerful *anti*-war neurosis.'

They looked at each other and laughed. Rivers said, 'You realize, don't you, that it's my duty to ... to try to change that? I can't pretend to be neutral.'

Sassoon's glance took in both their uniforms. 'No of course not.'

Page 15

2   'There's a limit to how warm you can feel about wallpaper.'

'Oh, we're back to that again, are we?

Prior turned away, hunching his shoulders. 'No-o.'

Rivers watched him for a while. 'Why do you think it has to be like that?'

'So that I ... I'm sorry. So that *the patient* can fantasize freely. So that *the patient* can turn you into whoever he wants you to be. Well, all right. I just think you might consider the possibility that *this* patient might want you to be *you*.'

'All right.'

'All right, what?'

'All right, I'll consider it.'

'I suppose most of them turn you into Daddy, don't they? Well, I'm a bit too old to be sitting on *Daddy*'s knee.'

'Kicking him on the shins every time you meet him isn't generally considered more mature.'

'I *see*. A negative transference. Is *that* what you think we've got?'

'I hope not.' Rivers couldn't altogether conceal his surprise. 'Where did you learn that term?'

'I can *read*.'

'Well, yes, I know, but its –'

'Not popular science? No, but then neither is this.'

He reached for the book beside his bed and held it out to Rivers. Rivers found himself holding a copy of *The Todas*. He stared for a moment at his own name on the spine. He told himself there was no reason why Prior shouldn't read one of his books, or all of them for that matter. There was no rational reason for him to feel uneasy. He handed the book back. 'Wouldn't you prefer something lighter? You are ill, after all.'

Prior leant back against his pillows, his eyes gleaming with amusement. 'Do you know, I *knew* you were going to say that. Now how did I know that?'

'I didn't realise you were interested in anthropology.'

'Why shouldn't I be?'

'No reason.'

Really, Rivers thought, Prior was cuckoo-backed to the point where normal conversation became almost impossible ...

'You have to *win* don't you?'

Prior stared intently at him. 'You know, you do a wonderful imitation of a stuffed shirt. And you're not like that at all, really, are you?'

Rivers took his glasses off and swept his hand across his eyes.

'*Mister Prior.*'

Page 64

3   When Bryce had finished, Brock turned to Rivers and said, 'What are you thinking of doing with him?'

'Well, I have been seeing him every day. I'm going to drop that now to three times a week.'

'Isn't that rather a lot? For someone who – according to you – has nothing wrong with him?'

'I shan't be able to persuade him to go back in less than that.'

'Isn't there a case for leaving him alone?'

'No.'

'I mean, simply by *being* here he's discredited. Discredited, disgraced, *apparently* lied to by his best friend? I'd've thought there was a case for letting him be.'

'No, there's no case,' Rivers said. 'He's a mentally and physically healthy man. It's *his* duty to go back, and it's *my* duty to see he does.'

'And you've no doubts about that at all?'

'I don't see the problem. I'm not going to give him electric shocks, or or subcutaneous injections of ether. I'm simply asking him to defend his position. Which he admits was reached largely on emotional grounds.'

'*Grief* at the death of his friends. *Horror* at the slaughter of everybody else's friends. It isn't clear to me why such emotions have to be ignored.'

'I'm not saying they should be ignored. Only that they mustn't be allowed to dominate.'

'The protopathic must know its place.'

Rivers looked taken aback. 'I wouldn't've put it quite like that.'

'Why not? It's your word. And Sassoon does seem to be a remarkably protopathic young man. Doesn't he? I mean from what you say, it's 'all or nothing' all the time. Happy warrior one minute. Bitter pacifist the next.'

'Precisely. He's completely inconsistent. And that's all the more reason to get him to *argue* the position –'

'Epicritically.'

'*Rationally.*'

Brock raised his hands and sat back in his chair. 'I hope you don't mind my playing devil's advocate?'

'Good heavens, no. The whole point of these meetings is to protect the patient.'

Brock smiled, one of his rare, thin, unexpectedly charming smiles. 'Is that what I was doing? I thought I was protecting you.'

Page 73

4   One evening he'd crept close to the open window of his father's study, sat down with his back to the wall and listened to the lesson in progress. Why he'd done this he couldn't now remember, except that it hadn't *felt* like eavesdropping, since he knew nothing private was likely to be said. Perhaps he'd just wanted to hear Dodgson put through the same routine he and the other boys were put through. Perhaps he'd wanted to see him cut down to size. Dodgson had just embarked on the sentence about the careful cat catching the mouse – a simple enough tale, but already, in Dodgson's mouth, threatening to become an epic. Rivers listened to his father's advice, the same advice, basically, that *he* got, though conveyed without that peculiar note of fraught patience. He thought suddenly, this is nonsense. It *doesn't* help to remember to keep your tongue down, it doesn't help to think about the flow of breath. So he'd thought, sweeping away his father's life work in a single minute as twelve-year-old boys are apt to do. He'd raised his head very cautiously above the window sill, and seen his father sitting behind the desk – this desk – his back to the window, clean pink neck showing above clean white collar, broad shoulders straining the cloth of his jacket. He stared at the back of his neck, at the neck of the man whom he had, in a way, just killed, and he didn't feel sad or guilty about it at all. He felt glad...

And yet, Rivers thought, running his hands across the scarred leather of the desk top, the relationship between father and son is never simple, and never over. Death certainly doesn't end it. In the past year he'd thought more about his father than he'd done since he was a child. Only recently it had occurred to him that if some twelve-year-old boy had crept up to his window at Craiglockhart, as he'd done to his father's window at Knowles Bank, he'd have seen a man sitting at a desk with his back to the window, listening to some patient, with a stammer far worse than Dodgson's, try and fail to reach the end of a sentence. Only that boy would not have been his son.

Page 155

5   He returned to his desk, and drew a stack of files towards him. He was writing brief notes on the patients who'd been Boarded that day, but this he could do almost automatically. His thoughts wandered as he wrote. He wasted no time wondering how he would feel if Siegfried were to be maimed or killed, because this was a possibility with any patient who returned to France. He'd faced that already, many times. If anything, he was amused by the irony of the situation, that he, who was in the business of changing people, should himself have been changed and by somebody who was clearly unaware of having done it.

It was a far deeper change, though, than merely coming to believe that a negotiated peace might be possible, and desirable. That at least it ought to be explored. He remembered telling Head how he had tried to change his life when he came back from Melanesia for the second time and how that attempt had failed. He'd gone on being reticent, introverted, reclusive. Of course it had been a very introverted, self-conscious attempt, and perhaps that was why it hadn't worked. Here in this building, where he had no time to be introverted or self-conscious, where he hardly had a moment to himself at all, the changes had taken place without his knowing. That was not Siegfried. That was all of them. Burns and Prior and Pugh and a hundred others. As a young man he'd been both by temperament and conviction, deeply conservative, and not merely in politics. Now, in middle age, the sheer extent of the *mess* seemed to be forcing him into conflict with the authorities over a very wide range of issues ... medical, military. Whatever. A society that devours its own young deserves no automatic or unquestioning allegiance. Perhaps the rebellion of the old might count for rather more than the rebellion of the young.

Page 248

A psychoanalyst's reading of Rivers

David Morgan, in his essay on 'Regeneration and the history of psychoanalysis', develops his interpretation of the character of Rivers more fully.

● Read his analysis of the development of Rivers' thinking about his patients and the war and how this relates to changes in ideas about trauma and neurosis.

The world of *Regeneration* is one in which a whole generation of men and their families were suddenly and horrifically confronted by what it meant to be a human being. Dr. Rivers as the objective medical man, also goes through a crisis, which can be seen as a metaphor for the loss of innocence suffered by his patients and his whole generation. At first his own medical discipline helps him to be objective. His medical training as an army officer allows him to feel he is doing right by his men; that he has to 'cure' them so that they can return to the trenches and almost certain death.

However, although the army probably saw the cure of these men as essential to get them back to the front, Rivers has the real task of managing his duty toward the army, but this comes more and more into conflict with him as a humane doctor and caring human being. When speaking to the hysterically paralysed Willard who is chastising himself for being a coward, Rivers says, 'It's true paralysis occurs because a man wants to save his life. He doesn't want to go forward, and take part in some hopeless attack. *But neither is he prepared to run away. ...* Paralysis is no use to a coward. A coward needs his legs.' (p112). Or when talking to Prior after the hypnosis that helped him remember the repressed trauma of finding a detached eye in the

trenches, Prior says 'there is a kind of person who breaks down ...' Rivers replies, 'I imagine most of us could if the pressure was bad enough. I know I could.'

Here we see Rivers becoming more sympathetic, relaxing his need to see his patients as merely ill and seeing them as displaying reasonable responses to untenable situations. One might ask the question, what stopped the other soldiers who were exposed to similar horrors from breaking down? What stopped the other psychiatrists, like Dr. Yealland, who uses electric shocks and coercion to cure his patients and send them back to the front, from seeing that it was cruel? The treatment of Callan in chapter 21 is a disturbing account of Dr. Yealland's unwitting brutality in treating the victims of the brutality of this war. It is a treatment that sees little meaning in the symptoms of the patients, only that they have to be repaired and sent back to the front like machines. It is this brutality that shakes Rivers' belief in what he is doing and why it becomes impossible for him to continue.

This is particularly well described in his relationship with Siegfried Sassoon. Throughout the book we see Sassoon, a poet, struggling with his conscience. He is clearly not a coward – he is in fact a hero – however he realises that the war is senseless and that his friends in the trenches are dying for nothing other than the arrogant wish of a few to continue the war whatever the cost. It his heroic struggle, with his wish on the one hand to be with his men, and on the other hand to stand against the stupidity of the war that impinges on Rivers. His own views of what he is trying to do are challenged. In the wrecks of his patients' minds he begins to see the senselessness of his own struggle to follow orders, yet he is also one of the few psychiatrists involved who works in a therapeutic way with his patients. In his treatment of them he allows them to talk to him, he treats them as people rather than as symptoms, he allows a relationship involving some dependence on him to develop and his patients find this helpful, and do feel better as a result. Because he gets to know his men, Rivers cannot deny the suffering that he sees around him. He becomes, like Sassoon, unable to turn a blind eye and pretend that it is all for the good of the war. This awareness causes him to struggle in his own conscience with what is right and wrong. This mirrors Sassoon's struggle to be with his friends or to use his position to speak out and maybe save lives. It is the capacity to feel deeply for others that begins to change Sassoon's and Rivers' minds about the war in which they are involved.

Rivers was becoming aware, as were Freud and others working with patients with psychological problems, that the patient and the physician are often struggling with similar problems around life and it is only the clinician's awareness of these problems in himself that can possibly help him to understand deeply his patient. In other words 'physician heal thyself'. This was a great struggle for Rivers. He says, 'The change he demanded of them – and by implication of himself – was not trivial. Fear, tenderness – these emotions were so despised that they could be admitted into consciousness only at the cost of redefining what it meant to be a man.' (page 48)

This is a great defining moment of the book because what River is conveying here is that, through working with men who have been classified as broken-down, he is faced with the reality that they are in fact dealing with repressed parts of themselves, their feelings and sensitivity that have for so long been trained out of them. This is a painful breakthrough of repressed parts of the self, but also as a result of the symptoms, a 'regeneration' of man as a possible feeling creature, rather than a machine to be repaired and sent out to kill or be killed. This insight paves the way for thinking about man as a psychological being with feelings and emotions.

A close reading of David Morgan's analysis

- In pairs, pick out:
  - five or six key phrases or sentences that help you to develop your thinking about Rivers and the way Barker explores ideas through his character
  - any parts of Morgan's argument that you have difficulty in following
  - any parts of Morgan's argument with which you strongly agree or disagree.

- As a whole class, talk about each pair's responses to the piece and clarify points of difficulty or disagreement.

Rivers and the other characters

One way of thinking about the other characters is in terms of their function in relation to Rivers. As Pat Barker says in her video interview, while all of the characters have their own stories, which create multiple plot lines in the novel, Rivers is the central focus and many of the other characters have an important function in revealing aspects of his character and development.

Rivers' is the central view point, and I would say that even about the next two volumes, where Prior becomes very prominent. [I wanted] the view point to correspond with my experience and the experience of the reader, which is that we were not combatants in the First World War. However much we learn about it, we have not had the experience, which is why, in the end, the perspective has to be Rivers'. And also, I think Rivers has a very sane perspective.

What all the minor characters do collectively, of course, is to give a very powerful sense of the pressures on Rivers: the different demands that are made on him by all these people at different times of the day, and the different ways in which the war traumatised people. It would not have been possible, I think, to focus more narrowly on Rivers and Sassoon, simply because you would have had a sense in which Rivers was simply sending the men back in a rather thoughtless way. Whereas, you have to be aware of how compassionate Rivers was, and how deeply he was aware of the suffering inflicted by the war.

- Take three or four of the characters listed on page 88 and talk about what each reveals to the reader about Rivers or contributes to the developments in his character. You could present your ideas in the form of a chart or spidergram.

Writing about Rivers

- Write your own analysis of the way in which Rivers, the character, enables Pat Barker to find an unusual angle on the First World War and explore the development of ideas about neurosis, psychoanalysis and the human mind. Make use of the ideas raised by David Morgan and Pat Barker herself but also add your own ideas and interpretations. For instance, you may want to say more about the way the other characters relate to Rivers and what this reveals.

William Rivers

Narrative viewpoint

Exploring a third person narrative

The narrative is written in the third person. Third person narratives:
- allow the writer to present events from more than one character's perspective
- know things that the characters themselves don't necessarily know
- make a connection with the reader that is distinct from any single character
- shift from one setting, episode or set of characters to another with maximum freedom.

Sometimes it is suggested that third person narratives don't allow you inside the thoughts and feelings of a character as powerfully as first person narratives.

● Look at the work on narrative viewpoint in the introductory section of the publication, to remind yourself of the effects of making different choices.

● Look at these short extracts from Chapter 4. Talk about the way in which the third person narrative is working here.

   – Whose viewpoint is it?
   – How is the viewpoint constructed?
   – Does the viewpoint shift?
   – What are the effects of the different methods of narration, such as dialogue, abbreviated sentences, reporting thoughts in the third person and so on?
   – In what ways is third person narration sometimes made more immediate? For instance, is there ever direct reporting of thoughts?
   – What is the effect of having these different kinds of narration even in just one chapter?

1   At intervals, as Rivers was doing his rounds as orderly officer for the day, he thought about this dream. It was disturbing in many ways. At first he'd been inclined to see the post-mortem apron as expressing no more than a lack of faith in *him*, or, more accurately, in his methods, since obviously any doctor who spends much time so attired is not meeting with uniform success on the wards. This lack of faith he knew to be present. Anderson, in his first interview, had virtually refused treatment, claiming that rest, the endless pursuit of golf balls, was all that he required.

page 31

2   'Your father's dead too, isn't he? How old were you when he died?'
   'Eight. But I hadn't seen much of him for some time before that. He left home when I was five.'
   'Do you remember him?'
   'A bit. I remember I used to like being kissed by him because his moustache tickled. My brothers went to the funeral. I didn't – apparently I was too upset. Probably just as well, because they came back terrified. It was a Jewish funeral, you see, and they couldn't understand what was going on. My elder brother said it was two old men in funny hats walking up and down saying jabber-jabber-jabber.'
   'You must've felt you'd lost him twice.'
   'Yes. We did lose him twice.'
   Rivers gazed out of the window. 'What difference would it have made, do you think, if your father had lived?'

A long silence. 'Better education.'

'But you went to Marlborough?'

'Yes, but I was *years* behind everybody else. Mother had this theory we were delicate and our brains shouldn't be taxed. I don't think I ever really caught up. I left Cambridge without taking my degree.'

'And then?'

Sassoon shook his head. 'Nothing much. Hunting, cricket. Writing poems. Not very good poems.'

'Didn't you find it all ... rather unsatisfying?'

'Yes, but I couldn't seem to see a way out. It was like being three different people, and they all wanted to go different ways.' A slight smile. 'The result was I went nowhere.'

Rivers waited.

'I mean, there was the riding, hunting, cricketing me, and then there was the ... the other side ... that was interested in poetry and music, and things like that. And I didn't seem able to ...' He laced his fingers. 'Knot them together.'

'And the third?'

'I'm sorry?'

'You said three.'

'Did I? I meant two.'

Ah. 'And then the war. You joined up on the first day.'

page 35

3   Burns stood at the window of his room. Rain had blurred the landscape, dissolving sky and hills together in a wash of grey. He loathed wet weather because then everybody stayed indoors, sitting around the patients' common room, talking, in strained or facetious tones, about the war the war the war.

A sharper gust of wind blew rain against the glass. Somehow or other he was going to have to get out. It wasn't forbidden, it was even encouraged, though he himself didn't go out much. He got his coat and went downstairs. On the corridor he met one of the nurses from his ward, who looked surprised to see him wearing his coat, but didn't ask where he was going.

At the main gates he stopped. Because he'd been inside so long, the possibilities seemed endless, though they resolved themselves quickly into two. *Into* Edinburgh, or away. And that was no choice at all: he knew he wasn't up to facing traffic.

page 37

Fact and fiction

Not only is *Regeneration* a novel based firmly on the historical events of the First World War, it also uses historical figures as characters and well-documented events as part of the plot. In her interview, Pat Barker is emphatic about the importance to her of being historically accurate.

> I'm primarily a novelist, and in that sense I'm interested in what makes the story, what allows the characters to develop. But at the same time, I read history at university, I didn't read literature, and so I do think I had drilled into me a sense that you don't fiddle with the facts. If a particular fact is inconvenient, and you would give anything for it to be different, too bad. You don't alter it merely because you're writing a novel. You accept that this is there, like a rock in the stream, and you find a creative way of going round it, but you don't change facts.

Some of the facts

William Rivers was a psychiatrist at Craiglockhart hospital during the First World War.
He did treat Siegfried Sassoon after Sassoon's 'A Soldier's Declaration.' This Declaration was a genuine document, read out in the House of Commons in 1917.
Sassoon met Wilfred Owen at the hospital and they often talked about their poetry. Sassoon did suggest amendments to Owen's famous poem, 'Anthem for Doomed Youth', which appear in Sassoon's handwriting on existing drafts of the poem.

Using the historical material

In this section you will be considering what Pat Barker has done with the historical material surrounding Rivers, Sassoon, Owen and their time at Craiglockhart.

● Look at these non-fiction and historical documents relating to the events at Craiglockhart. Read each one in turn. Talk about your initial ideas about how they relate to the novel. Then try to pair each text with a short extract from the novel and compare in detail the factual, historical texts with their treatment as fiction.

● Share your pairings as a class and talk about how Barker's fictional approach compares with the historical texts.
For instance:
 – has she tried to absorb anything of the voices of the figures themselves
 – is her 'telling' self-consciously fictional or literary, or does it avoid drawing attention to itself as a story
 – how does the third person narration affect the telling
 – in dealing with the 'real' people, how closely does she seem to stick to the 'true' story
 – how does she shape the incidents to engage the reader in the ways that fiction does?

1   **'An Address on the Repression of War Experience'**
    The process of repression does not cease when some shock or strain has removed the soldier from the scene of warfare, but it may take an active part in the maintenance of the neurosis. New symptoms often arise in hospital or at home which are not the immediate and necessary consequence of the war experience, but are due to repression of painful memories and thoughts, or of unpleasant affective states arising out of reflection concerning this experience. It is with the repression of the hospital and of the home rather than with the repression of the trenches that I deal in this paper. I propose to illustrate by a few sample cases some of the effects which may

be produced by repression and the line of action by which these effects may be remedied. I hope to show that many of the most trying and distressing symptoms from which the subjects of war neurosis suffer are not the necessary result of the strains and shocks to which they have been exposed in warfare, but are due to the attempt to banish from the mind distressing memories of warfare or painful affective states which have come into being as a result of their war experience.

William Rivers

2   **The Complete Memoirs of George Sherston**

I would give a lot for a few gramophone records of my talks with Rivers. All that matters is my remembrance of the great and good man who gave me his friendship and guidance. I can visualize him, sitting at his table in the late summer twilight, with his spectacles pushed up on his forehead and his hands clasped in front of one knee; always communicating his integrity of mind; never revealing that he was weary as he must often have been after long days of exceptionally tiring work on those war neuroses which demanded such an exercise of sympathy and detachment combined. Remembering all that, and my egotistic unawareness of the possibility that I was often wasting his time and energy, I am consoled by the certainty that he did, on the whole, find me a refreshing companion. He liked me and he believed in me.

Siegfried Sassoon

3   **Siegfried's Journey, 1916-1920**

One morning at the beginning of August, when I had been at Craiglockhart War Hospital about a fortnight, there was a gentle knock on the door of my room and a young officer entered. Short, dark-haired, and shyly hesitant, he stood for a moment before coming across to the window, where I was sitting on my bed cleaning my golf clubs. A favourable first impression was made by the fact that he had under his arm several copies of *The Old Huntsman*. He had come, he said, hoping that I would be so gracious as to inscribe them for himself and some of his friends. He spoke with a slight stammer, which was no unusual thing in that neurosis-pervaded hospital. My leisurely, commentative method of inscribing the books enabled him to feel more at home with me. He had a charming honest smile, and his manners – he stood at my elbow rather as though conferring with a superior officer – were modest and ingratiating. He gave me the names of his friends first. When it came to his own I found myself writing one that has since gained a notable place on the roll of English poets – Wilfred Owen. I had taken an instinctive liking to him, and felt that I could talk freely. During the next half-hour or more I must have spoken mainly about my book and its interpretations of the war. He listened eagerly, questioning me with reticent intelligence. It was only when he was departing that he confessed to being a writer of poetry himself, though none of it had yet appeared in print.

Siegfried Sassoon

4   **Extract from *Goodbye to All That***

The thought of France nearly drove him dotty sometimes. Down in Kent he could hear the guns thudding ceaselessly across the Channel, on and on, until he didn't know whether he wanted to rush back and die with the First Battalion, or stay in England and do what he could to prevent the war going on. But both courses were hopeless. To go back and get killed would be only playing to the gallery – the wrong gallery – and he could think of no means of doing any effective preventive work at home. His name had gone in for an officer-cadet battalion appointment in England, which would keep him safe if he pleased; but it seemed a dishonourable way out.

Siegfried sends him a copy of his 'Soldier's Declaration'.

This filled me with anxiety and unhappiness. I entirely agreed with Siegfried about the 'political errors and insincerities' and thought his action magnificently courageous. But more things had to be considered than the strength of our case against the politicians. In the first place, he was in no proper physical condition to suffer the penalty which the letter invited: namely to be court-martialled, cashiered, and imprisoned. I found myself most bitter with the pacifists who had encouraged him to make this gesture. I felt that, not being soldiers, they could not understand what it cost Siegfried emotionally. It was wicked that he should have to face the consequences of his letter on top of those Quadrangle and Fontaine-les-Croiselles experiences. I also realized the inadequacy of such a gesture. Nobody would follow his example, either in England or in Germany. The war would inevitably go on and on until one side or the other cracked …

Graves successfully intervenes to try to get Siegfried a medical board, to prevent him from being court-martialled.

Next, I had to rig the medical board. I applied for permission to give evidence as a friend of the patient. There were three doctors on the board – a regular RAMC colonel and major, and a 'duration of the war' captain. I very soon realized that the colonel was patriotic and unsympathetic; but ignorant; and the captain a competent nerve-specialist, right-minded, and my only hope. I had to go through the whole story again, treating the colonel and major with the utmost deference, but using the captain as an ally to break down their scruples. Much against my will, I had to appear in the role of the patriot distressed by the mental collapse of a brother-in-arms – a collapse directly due to his magnificent exploits in the trenches. I mentioned Siegfried's 'hallucinations' of corpses strewn along on Picadilly. The irony of having to argue to these mad old men that Siegfried was not sane! Though conscious of a betrayal of truth, I acted jesuitically. Being in nearly as bad a state of nerves as Siegfried myself, I burst into tears three times during my statement. Captain McDowell, who proved to be a well-known Harley Street psychologist, played up well. As I went out, he said to me: 'Young man, you ought to be before this board yourself.' I prayed that when Siegfried came into the boardroom after me he would not undo my work by appearing too sane. But McDowell argued his seniors to my view.

Macartney-Filgate detailed me as Siegfried's escort to a convalescent home for neurasthenics at Craiglockhart, near Edinburgh. Siegfried and I both thought this a great joke, especially when I missed the train and he reported to 'Dottyville,' as he called it, without me. At Craiglockhart, Siegfried came under the care of Professor W.H.R. Rivers, whom we now met for the first time, though we already knew him as a leading Cambridge neurologist, ethnologist, and psychologist.

Rupert Graves

War fictions

There have been a number of novels written about the First World War. A close reading of extracts of these novels reveals very different approaches to the subject.

● Look at the extracts below and use the prompts to help you consider the decisions the writers have made.

- What does the writer seem most interested in?
- Are accounts of the trenches presented directly or as memory?
- Whose point of view is it written from?
- Are the main characters soldiers? What difference does this make?
- How is the horror of the war handled?
- Does the writing confirm your existing understandings about the First World War or undermine them?

● Think about the extracts in relation to *Regeneration*. What do they make you notice about the way *Regeneration* is written and the choices that Pat Barker has made? Your starting-point might be to make a list of statements such as the one below:

Whereas *All Quiet on the Western Front* is written in the first person, *Regeneration* is a third person narrative. The effect of this is to …

Birdsong

The three men lay close together. They feared shell wounds more than bullets because they had seen the damage they did. A direct hit would obliterate all physical evidence that a man had existed; a lesser one would rip pieces from him; even a contained wound brought greater damage to the tissue of the body than a bullet. Infection or gangrene often followed.

A sharp wailing began a few yards down the trench. It was a shrill, demented sound that cut through even the varying noises of gunfire. A youth called Tipper ran along the duckboards, then stopped and lifted his face to the sky. He screamed again, a sound of primal fear that shook the others who heard it. His thin body was rigid and they could see the contortions of his facial muscles beneath the skin. He was screaming for his home.

Byrne and Wilkinson began swearing at him.

'Help me,' said Stephen to Reeves. He went and took the boy's arm and tried to sit him down on the firestep. Reeves gripped him from the other side. His eyes were fixed on the sky and neither Stephen nor Reeves was able to unlock the muscles of his neck and make him look downward.

Tipper's face appeared to have lost all its circulation. The whites of his eyes, only a few inches from Stephen's face, bore no red tracery of blood vessels; there was only a brown circle with a dilated pupil floating in an area of white which was enlarged by the spasmodic opening of the eye. The pupil seemed to grow blacker and wider, so that the iris lost all light and sense of life.

With no idea of where he was, the boy repeatedly and imploringly called out some private word that might have been a pet name for his father or mother. It was a noise of primitive fear. Stephen felt a sudden loosening of compassion, which he quelled as quickly as he could.

'Get him out, ' he said to Reeves. 'I don't want this here. You and Wilkinson, get him to the MO.'

'Yes, sir.' Reeves and Wilkinson dragged the rigid body to the communication trench.

Stephen was shaken. This eruption of natural fear brought home how unnatural was the existence they were leading; they did not wish to be reminded of normality. By the time he returned to his dugout, he was angry. If the pretence began to break, then it would take lives with it.

There seemed to be no way in which they could confront this dread. At Ypres and in other actions they had been able to prepare themselves to die, but the shellfire unmanned them all again. Men who had prepared themselves to walk into machine guns or defend their trenches to the last could not face death in this shape. They pretended that it was more than this; it was the evidence of what they had seen. Reeves had searched for his brother but had found no trace to bury, not a lock of hair, not even a piece of boot. He told Stephen this with bitterness and disbelief. The shell that had taken him was of a size that had to be loaded by crane from a light railway; after flying six miles at altitude it had left a crater large enough to house a farm with outbuildings. It was no wonder, Reeves said, that there was no trace of his brother. 'I wouldn't mind,' he said, 'but he was my own flesh and blood.'

Sebastian Faulks

Strange Meeting

Barton stepped out of the dugout and looked up. For the first time in weeks the sky was clear and glittering with the points of stars, a full moon shone above the ridge. The frost was thin and here and there it caught in the pale light on the barbed wire, tin canisters, helmets, and gleamed. The night cold had taken the edge off the smell of decay and the air was sharp and metallic in Barton's nostrils. He moved quietly along the trench. In the next dugout, twenty or so men slept under great-coats, a jumble of arms and feet. It was very still, no gunfire, no flares.

'Sir?'

'Hello, Parkin. All right?'

'All quiet, sir, yes. Funny that.'

'Hm.' Barton leaned against the side of the trench.

'You haven't been in a big show yet, have you, sir?'

'No. Have you?'

'No.'

Parkin was a year younger than himself, one of the eleven children of a cobbler – which fact occasioned three or four jokes a day about his living in a shoe. He took it with good humour, as though he were still among boys at school, entirely used to the amusement it afforded them. Jokes among the company had become either simple or obscene and childish, as the life became more exhausting and tedious.

Barton said, 'So we feel the same about tomorrow, then.'

'Do we, sir? How's that?'

'A bit queasy.'

Parkin looked relieved, nodded. 'I was thinking before you came along sir – it's all right here at the moment. Quiet. A bit chilly but I can cope with that. There's a touch of something in the air – I don't know, maybe it's just that the bloody rain's stopped. But it's been reminding me of making bonfires and getting ready for Christmas, you know? I was feeling quite happy, just watching out and thinking. Then I got that feeling – like when you wake up and you know something a bit unpleasant's due to happen and for the time being you've forgotten what. I thought – what's up? Then I remembered.'

'I know.'

'Still – we're ready, aren't we? We've got the lot up here and we know what we've got to do. It's just a question of getting on and doing it. Maybe we'll be over there tomorrow night, they'll have run for it and we'll be kipping in Jerry's feather beds. They have everything in those trenches of theirs you know, sir – so they say, anyway. All home comforts. They dug themselves in good and proper.'

Barton watched the man's face as he talked so quickly, talked himself into some sort of reassurance, he saw the twitching at the corner of his eye, the way his mouth moved. He thought that he ought to say something to him, provide the expected words of comfort and support. He could say nothing. He knew. Parkin knew.

'Do you want to turn the lamp on?' Hilliard said.

'I thought you were asleep.'

'No, I was waiting for you. If you want to read ...'

'No.'

Barton lay down, still in his greatcoat. 'You're right. "Not a mouse stirring".'

'It often happens like this, it's uncanny. I remember it in July.'

'But they must know we're up to something.'

'Oh yes. Though that fact is never obvious to High Command, whose faith in the Element of Surprise in attack is really very touching. And quite unshakeable.'

'John, shall I stop feeling so bloody afraid?'

'Things will get so busy you'll have no time for it, that's all I can promise you. But this is the worst bit, this building up of tension.'

'Like the dentist.'

'Rather a pale analogy – but yes.'

'Shall we be due for leave afterwards, do you suppose?'

'Surely. We might even get home for Christmas.'

'Both of us?'

'Anything is possible. Don't bank on it though.'

'I'd like you to come to us for Christmas but your family would object, I imagine.'

'I could come for part of the time. But really we had better not start building castles in Spain.'

'John, I want you to come and see it all.'

'Yes.'

'I want to take you everywhere, show you everything – oh, it doesn't matter if it doesn't come off for Christmas, we'll do it sometime. There's so much ... I want it all to look right and be right – I want you to like them all.'

'Will they like me is much more to the point.'

'Oh, of course they will.'

'Of course?'

'Yes, because they couldn't help it and because you're my friend – and because really, they like nearly everyone.'

'So do you, don't you?'

'More or less, I suppose.'

'Has it always been like that? Has it always been so easy for you to love people? To get on with them, to bring them out, say the right things at the right time? Have you always made friends as you've done out here?'

'I've never really thought about it. But that part is easy you know. The big outer circle of friends.'

'Is it?'

'Oh yes. It's the other which is the real luck – what we have. That's another matter altogether. Things don't happen like this often in a lifetime.'

'Have you – do you have other friends who – is it the same with anyone else?'

'No.'

Hilliard felt a rush of joy and his mouth was filled up with the words he wanted to say, his head rang with them and he could say nothing.

Footsteps went by in the trench outside, voices came softly.

Then silence again.

In the end they slept.

Susan Hill

All Quiet on the Western Front

They have taken us farther back than usual to a field depot so that we can be re-organized. Our company needs more than a hundred reinforcements.

In the meantime, when we are off duty, we loaf around. After a couple of days Himmelstoss comes up to us. He has had the bounce knocked out of him since he has been in the trenches and wants to get on good terms with us. I am willing, because I saw how he brought Haie Westhus in when he was hit in the back. Besides he's decent enough to treat us in the canteen when we are out of funds. Only Tjaden is still reserved and suspicious.

But he is won over, too, when Himmelstoss tells us that he is taking the place of the sergeant-cook who has gone on leave. As a proof he produces on the spot two pounds of sugar for us and a half-pound of butter specially for Tjaden. He even sees to it that we are detailed the next two or three days to the cook-house for potato and turnip peeling. The grub he gives us there is real officers' fare.

Thus momentarily we have the two things a soldier needs for contentment: good food and rest. That's not much when one comes to think of it. A few years ago we would have despised ourselves terribly. But now we are almost happy. It is all a matter of habit – even the front-line.

Habit is the explanation of why we seem to forget things so quickly. Yesterday we were under fire, today we act the fool and go foraging through the countryside, tomorrow we go up to the trenches again. We forget nothing really. But so long as we have to stay here in the field, the front-line days, when they are past, sink down in us like a stone; they are too grievous for us to be able to reflect on them at once. If we did that, we should have been destroyed long ago. I soon found out this much: – terror can be endured so long as a man simply ducks; – but it kills, if a man thinks about it.

Just as we turn into animals when we go up to the line, because that is the only thing which brings us through safely, so we turn into wags and loafers when we are resting. We can do nothing else, it is a sheer necessity. We want to live at any price; so we cannot burden ourselves with feelings which, though they might be ornamental enough in peace-time, would be out of place here. Kemmerich is dead, Haie Westhus is dying, they will have a job with Hans Kramer's body at the Judgement Day, piecing it together after a direct hit; Martens has no legs any more, Meyer is dead, Max is dead, Beyer is dead, Hämmerling is dead, there are a hundred and twenty wounded men lying somewhere or other; it is a damnable business, but what has it do with us now – we live. If it were possible for us to save them, then it would be seen how much we cared – we would have a shot at it though we went under ourselves; for we can be damned quixotic when we like; fear we do not know much about – terror of death, yes; but that is a different matter, that is physical.

But our comrades are dead, we cannot help them, they have their rest – and who knows what is waiting for us? We will make ourselves comfortable and sleep, and eat as much as we can stuff into our bellies, and drink and smoke so that the hours are not wasted.

Erich Maria Remarque

History as story

While *Regeneration* and other war fictions are clearly novels and John Keegan's *The First World War* on page 79 is clearly a non-fiction book about history, it would be wrong to suggest that the divide between fiction and history is rigid. Most contemporary historians recognise the fact that they are constructing a 'story' out of the data available to them and that every historian's 'story' is inevitably subjective – an 'interpretation' of historical material, privileging certain aspects and leaving out others.

● Read the quotation by Marc Trachtenberg below, which takes this idea a bit further.

> Increasingly, the old ideal of historical objectivity is dismissed out of hand. The very notion of 'historical truth' is now often considered hopelessly naïve. Instead, the tendency is for people to insist that all interpretation is to be understood in essentially political terms. If objectivity is a myth, how can our understanding of the past be anything but an artifact of our political beliefs? Indeed, if all interpretation is political anyway, then why not give free rein to one's own political views? Why not use whatever power one happens to have to 'privilege' one's own brand of history?'
>
> **Marc Trachtenberg**

● Think about this quotation in relation to *Regeneration*. What version of the First World War is offered by Pat Barker? For instance, do you agree that this is one aspect of her version of history:

> Pat Barker takes a feminist angle on history, focusing more than many historians might on the effects of the First World War on women and work, women's relationships with each other and power relationships between women and men.

● Share your ideas as a whole class, talking about the evidence and ideas in the novel that support your views.

Multiple versions of history

In telling different characters' stories, Pat Barker allows different versions of history to stand alongside each other or sometimes challenge each other. This is one of the ways in which fiction can tell a more complex, multi-faceted 'story' than history. For instance, the character of Rivers is shown to change in the course of the novel, as both his version of the war, and his view of the world, are challenged by the views of other characters.

● Read the opening of Chapter 5, where Rivers meets Prior for the first time (pages 41-43) and the opening of Chapter 6, where they have a second consultation (pages 49-53).

● Talk about Rivers' and Prior's view of each other in each of these meetings, focusing particularly on the differences and antagonisms between them and the ways in which they respond to each other on each occasion.

An alternative reading – fiction suffering from the weight of history

● Read this comment by Lavinia Greenlaw. Talk about what she seems to be saying and how far you believe this to be a problem in *Regeneration*.

The authenticity of history is useful to writers of fiction. It can be challenged or invoked; and its scale can be adjusted to amplify or to diminish human drama, either way providing props, backdrops and special effects at comparatively little imaginative cost. The dangers are obvious: fiction is authenticated by its evidence of research-details of the real place, people, technology. Anecdotes and arcane practices impress us primarily because they are 'real'.

Lavinia Greenlaw, *The New Republic*, Washington April 29, 96

Blending story and history

While Pat Barker wrote about many historical characters (Rivers, Sassoon, Owen, Bryce, Henry and Ruth Head and so on), she also wove into the story fictional characters, based on case studies she had read. Of these David Burns and Billy Prior are the most fully developed.

Lavinia Greenlaw, has said of the novel:

> It is where Barker is less self-consciously factual, less awed by her research and more confident of her fiction, that the books come to life ... the belligerent Billy Prior, a working-class officer or 'temporary gentleman' is intelligent and articulate, aspiring to amorality but with a weakness for big ideas. He proves a perturbing patient for Rivers, whom he mimics, teases and confronts, making for far more interesting reading than the mutually admiring and self-consciously understated exchanges of Rivers and Sassoon. The contrast between the two characters is instructive: it is as if Barker knew how Sassoon should speak but can let Prior find out for himself.

Herbert Mittgang's view is quite the opposite.

> ... Ms. Barker makes the conversations between her poets and the doctors at the hospital sound absolutely authentic. We are aware that she is inventing dialogue for her characters, but it is informed invention. If this isn't how they actually spoke, then it's surely how they might have: with wit, irony and understated seriousness.

Pat Barker herself said in her interview:

> It was interesting, especially perhaps in the next book, *The Eye in the Door*, writing about Rivers and Prior, because of the need to be fair to Rivers and the need to be historically accurate all the time. It was often a very great relief to me when I got to a point where I could write about Prior, and invent freely. And Prior is no respecter of persons, so he was a delight to write about. But after a few chapters of being in Prior's mind, I found that I couldn't wait to get back to Rivers, to get that sanity, that moral perspective, because Prior is not restful to write about. He's fun, but he's not restful.

● Look at the short extracts from the novel re-printed on pages 108 and 109. The first involves just historical characters; the second involves just fictional characters; the third involves both. Talk about the style of writing in these extracts, using the questions suggested here as prompts.

- Do you notice any differences?
- Where they appear together, how effectively are the historical and fictional characters blended together?
- Do you think these extracts are representative of the rest of the book, or could you find other examples of Barker's style that are quite different?

- From your close work on these extracts from the novel, talk about whether you support the view taken by Greenlaw or Mittgang, or whether you have an alternative view of your own? For example, you might think the style of these conversations between Rivers and Sassoon expresses well the nature of their relationship.

- Talk about which characters in the novel you personally found most memorable, interesting or powerful.

1   'Did you sleep well?'

'Very well, thank you.'

'You look rested. I enjoyed meeting Captain Graves.'

'Yes, I gather you found it quite informative.'

'*Ah*.' Rivers paused in the act of opening the file. 'You mean he told me something you'd rather I didn't know?'

'No, not necessarily. Just something I might have preferred to tell you myself.' A moment's silence, then Sassoon burst out, 'What I can't understand is how somebody of Graves's intelligence can can can have such a shaky grasp of of *rhetoric*.'

Rivers smiled. 'You were going to kill Lloyd George rhetorically, were you?'

'I wasn't going to kill him at all. I said I *felt* like killing him, but it was no use, because they'd only shut me up in a lunatic asylum, "like Richard Dadd of glorious memory". There you are, *exact words*.' He looked round the room.

'Though as things have turned out –'

'This is *not* a lunatic asylum. You are *not* locked up.'

'Sorry.'

'What you're really saying is that Graves took you too seriously.'

'It's not just that. It suits him to attribute everything I've done to to to to ... a state of mental breakdown, because then he doesn't have to ask himself any awkward questions. Like why he agrees with me about the war and does nothing about it.'

Rivers waited a few moments. 'I know Richard Dadd was a painter. What else did he do?'

A short silence. 'He murdered his father.'

Pages 33-34

2   They took their time walking to the sea. At first he was disappointed, it was so crowded. Men with trousers rolled up to show knobbly legs, handkerchiefs knotted over sweating scalps, women with skirts tucked up to reveal voluminous bloomers, small children screaming as the damp sand was towelled off their legs. Everywhere people swirling their tongues round ice-cream cones, biting into candy-floss, licking rock, sucking fingers, determined to squeeze the last ounce of pleasure from the day. In his khaki, Prior moved among them like a ghost. Only Sarah connected him to the jostling crowd, and he put his hand around her, clasping her tightly, though at that moment he felt no stirring of desire. He said, 'You wouldn't think there was a war on, would you?'

They walked down to the water's edge. He felt quite callous towards her now, even as he drew her towards him and matched his stride to hers. She belonged with the pleasure-seeking crowds. He both envied and despised her, and was quite coldly determined to *get* her. They owed him something, all of them, and she should pay. He glanced at her. 'Shall we walk along?'

Page 127-8

3   Rivers sat back in his chair. 'Would you like to tell me something about that early part?'

'No.'

'But you do remember it?'

'Doesn't mean I want to talk about it.' He looked round the room. 'I don't see why it has to *be* like this anyway.'

'Like what?'

'All the questions from *you*, all the answers from *me*. Why can't it be both ways?'

'Look, Mr Prior, if you went to the doctor with bronchitis and he spent half the consultation time telling you about his lumbago, you would not be pleased. Would you?'

'No, but if I went to my doctor *in despair* it might help to know he at least understood the *meaning* of the word.'

'Are you in despair?'

Prior sighed, ostentatiously impatient.

'You know, I talk to a lot of people who *are* in despair or very close to it, and my experience is that they don't *care* what the doctor feels. That's the whole point about despair, isn't it? That you turn in on yourself.'

'Well, all I can say is I'd rather talk to a real person than a a strip of empathetic wallpaper.'

Rivers smiled. 'I like that.'

Prior glared at him.

Pages 50-51

A focus on Prior

When interviewed, Pat Barker said of Billy Prior,

> I was presented with a situation where virtually everybody in that hospital revered Rivers almost to the point of idolatry, if not actually to the point of idolatry. And even Sassoon, who takes the opposite point of view about the war, nonetheless, loves and respects Rivers as a kind of father figure. And, this is all very nice, of course, but it doesn't make for a very dramatic conflict-laden atmosphere, and it doesn't create situations in which Rivers can reveal himself as a human being. So, I created Prior. Every single aspect of Prior's character is designed to elucidate something from Rivers. He's a human being born to get up Rivers' nose and irritate him. So he's bisexual, which is very lightly sketched in, but I think it's there: he's sexually probing, he's sexually seductive, he's always probing into the inner reaches of Rivers' private life. He's working class, so Rivers, being a man of his time, of course, was what we would probably call a snob, he had ideas about what kind of person should be an officer in the British army, and it was not Billy Prior. And at the same time, he was a man of sufficient integrity to be slightly ashamed of this reaction. So, immediately, you have this very conflict-laden atmosphere between Rivers and Prior, in which they can bounce off each other. And, in a larger sense, that is the relationship throughout the book, throughout the trilogy, between the historical characters and the fictional characters. It's almost as if you can take the historical character, and by putting him against the background of a particular fictional character, you throw some of his speeches into sharper relief.

- Track the development of Prior's character, by choosing six or seven extracts at different stages in the novel, to show:
  - how he changes during the novel
  - how the reader's view of him is constructed and is changed during the novel.
  (The section on Rivers on pages 91-95, gives you a model for this.)

- Compare the extracts you have chosen with someone else's and present to each other your thinking about the way in which Prior is presented during the novel.

A debate about Prior
- Working in pairs, choose one side of each of the arguments below, drawing up ideas and evidence to support your case. Debate the arguments with another pair.

Unlike Rivers, Prior doesn't change. He's fundamentally the same man at the end of the novel as he was at the beginning. The real 'regeneration' is Rivers'.

While Rivers is supposed to be the main character in the novel, the reader is most attracted to and interested in the character of Prior.

Prior is the most important character in the novel, in terms of the themes he raises.

One of Pat Barker's greatest achievements in this novel is the way that she integrates historical and fictional characters. This is reflected in the creation of the character of Prior.

Structure – the glue that holds the novel together

Regeneration is very much a novel about ideas. As Pat Barker says in her interview, the normal plot structures do not really apply:

> Life at Craiglockhart was inherently uneventful, I think. It was intended to be uneventful, because, after all, they were there to rest. So, apart from the three monthly medical boards, virtually nothing happens. And, of course, this is difficult. But I found that there is a kind of drama within the therapeutic conversation, that it's not people chatting together, it is very much a focused exchange, with its own peaks and troughs, and its own nuances of meaning underneath, and the subtext and all the rest of it. In that sense, it's alike, but at the same time different from court room dialogue, which, once again, is far more focused than normal conversational exchange ever is.

In this kind of novel, the techniques for holding it together and giving it a coherent development and structure, are particularly important. Listed below are some of the strategies used by Barker.

● Consider each one in turn. Add any other ideas of your own.

The central metaphor of 'regeneration'

A metaphor can act as a motif, or organising principle for a novel. In this case the metaphor of nerve regeneration is used to unify many of the key ideas.

● Talk about all of the ways in which the novel returns to the idea of regeneration, thinking about:
  – the plot
  – the characters
  – the ideas about war, neurosis and healing.

Oppositions and thematic patterns
● Think back to the work you did on oppositions on page 87. Consider how these oppositions help the reader to make sense of the characters and plot and give shape to them.

Structuring dialogues and changing viewpoints
Much of *Regeneration* is a series of conversations, often simply the consultations between doctor and patient that form the patients' therapy. However, they are not just formless dialogues. Pat Barker shapes them into a development and interweaves them with other kinds of narrative and plot developments.

● Look at the chapter summary on pages 125 to 126. Annotate it to show patterns in the way Barker structures the novel. Think about the questions below, while you are doing your annotations.

– How does the four part structure work? What marks the end of each part? Is it an event (such as Prior meeting Sarah, or Sassoon being given permission to return to France) or is it used to mark a major shift in a character's thinking?

– How does Barker shift the character focus? Is each chapter about a different character, in strict rotation, or does she move backwards and forwards? Are links made at the changeover or does she make a sudden switch? What does she do to stop the reader from becoming confused by the shifting viewpoints?

Language – a central motif

Language is, in many different ways, an important issue in the novel, not just in terms of the language the writer uses to develop her ideas.

● Look at the different ways in which language occurs as an idea in its own right in the novel, which are listed below. Talk about the implications of each for the novel as a whole and write notes about your ideas.

> There are many examples of mutism in the book.

> The novel opens with Sassoon's written (verbal) protest.

> Many of the men stammer.

> Rivers has a stammer.

> Yealland's patient is forcibly 'cured' of mutism.

> Much of the novel consists of 'talk' – psychoanalysis is a 'talking' therapy.

> Memory is uncovered through language.

> Poetry is talked about a lot and extracts are included in the novel.

> The language of the Officers, soldiers, Medical Boards and working women is strongly evoked.

> Rivers reflects on silence, speech and protest.

● Are there any other motifs running through the book that give it shape and pattern? For instance, what is the function of the poetry quoted in the novel?

Interpretations by other readers

Individual interpretations

Every reader has his or her own unique perspective on what he or she reads.

- On your own, without talking to anyone else, write a paragraph summarising your ideas and feelings about *Regeneration* – what you found particularly interesting or enjoyable or engaging and which aspects of the book affected or impressed you most.

- Listen to each others' summaries and talk about the differences between them.

- Now read David Morgan's summary of his response to the novel. He is bringing to bear on his reading a range of different things: his previous experience of reading novels; his interest and expertise in psychoanalysis, drawn from his working life as a psychoanalyst, and his general interest in world events and history. What he chooses to focus on is not the same as many other readers, and may differ substantially from your reading.

- Talk about what you find interesting about his personal response to the novel. How does his interpretation compare with your own?

David Morgan's reading

Rivers was beginning to explore the idea that symptoms had meaning that indicated deeper problems that needed to be understood in the context of a therapeutic relationship. As someone working with people in this way, I find the treatment of this an extremely impressive part of the book. Barker captures the real struggle of patient and therapist, particularly the threat to the therapist's own way of thinking and stability. This was a move to a new way of thinking about people. Sensitivity and feelings did not have to be repressed or institutionalised out of people. In fact they represent perhaps what was so essential about human beings, their capacity to love deeply, restrain their violent wishes towards others and be creative and do good works, rather than be preoccupied with power and dominance. Barker demonstrates beautifully Rivers' struggle to encompass his patients' suffering and his own crisis of confidence. Maybe it's only when we have struggled with the wilder parts of man that make it impossible to live together, that we will be able to see a world that is not dominated by human destructiveness. Until then it will depend on political intervention and military strategy, as a last resort. Men will have to continue to be traumatised because the likes of Hitler and Stalin, or more recently, Saddam Hussein, will not ever go and see anyone about their problems. Just think of the lives that might have been saved if they had been able to understand what drove them to act in the ways that they did.

Reading *Regeneration* from different critical positions

Some readers and critics deliberately choose to read from a particular critical position. They use this critical position to inform, extend or even take the place of their own individual, personal responses.

- Look at the readings on page 114. They are slightly exaggerated readings from different positions. Talk about each in turn. Decide whether you agree or disagree with each one.

- Try to attach to each a broad label, indicating what the reading suggests about what the writer of it is most interested in. For instance is it, broadly:
  - a feminist reading
  - a Marxist reading
  - a psychoanalytic reading
  - a 'queer' reading? *

Reading 1

Regeneration is about the process of analysis. It's about healing through memory. It questions whether the men's analysis of their memories helps them to recovery. However, it questions whether, in the instance of the First World War, repression might not have been better and whether healing was a way of silencing protest.

On another level, the process for our culture is a similar one. We have gone through the same processes of repressing what we haven't been able to collectively face up to about the First World War. *Regeneration* as a novel has a role in exposing what has been repressed about the past.

Reading 2

While the conversations between Sassoon and Rivers are apparently the focal point of the novel, the real centre of the novel is the fictional character of Billy Prior and the sets of oppositions that cluster round him and his relationship with Rivers. It is Prior who challenges Rivers' (and the reader's preconceptions) and the confrontations between them, rooted as they are in class and cultural difference, provide both the dramatic tension and the focus for Barker's ideas about war and class.

Reading 3

One of the key themes of *Regeneration* is the question of masculinity, which is thrown into sharp relief by the context of the First World War. Challenges to the traditional divisions between what constitutes male and female behaviour are explored. Beneath the surface of the novel is the undercurrent of sexual tension, in the relationships between the main characters: Rivers and Sassoon, Sassoon and Owen, Rivers and Prior. Yet, in this novel, Pat Barker only hints at feelings that are never fully explored (and this, in a novel that is all about uncovering repressed feelings!) Homosexuality is only explicitly considered in the novel as a theoretical discussion, though in the second two books of the trilogy Prior's bisexuality, in particular, is more thoroughly and interestingly developed.

Reading 4

Although the novel takes as its subject matter the classic male themes of war and masculinity, it is written from a standpoint which questions gender roles and reflects on the changes in concepts of masculine and feminine behaviour brought about by the cultural and political watershed of the First World War. It is the effects of this war on 'men' and 'women' that is of prime interest to the writer, rather than on people. She uses her characters to look at the way the repressive, stiff-upper-lip culture of the pre-war years, led to an inability to recover from the trauma of war. Through her female characters, she also explores the way in which the war changed the lives of women and the sexual and power relationships between women.

- Choose one of the statements to work on. Make it the starting-point for an essay. Find evidence from the novel to support or contradict each element in the argument. Add to, qualify or radically alter the argument with ideas of your own and find evidence to support these new ideas.

* In the past the term 'queer' has been used as a derogatory term but in recent years it has been reclaimed by gay men and women and applied to criticism that explores issues of homosexuality in texts.

Reviewers' responses to *Regeneration*

- Look at these reviews and extracts of reviews of the novel. For each one, use these prompts to help you identify what the critic is saying and what kind of position the critic is writing from:
  - what the critic is mainly interested in (e.g. character, plot, narrative technique, reader-responses, contextual issues and so on)
  - to what extent the reviewer is describing, analysing or evaluating the novel
  - what kind of audience is suggested by the tone, length and focus of the review
  - what the reviewer's comments suggest about his or her expectations of a novel and how far these match your own
  - how far you agree with the main points the reviewer is making.

- Write a detailed response to one of the reviews, in which you explore how it works as a piece of critical writing, as well as commenting in detail on the arguments it raises about the novel. Use evidence from both the review and the novel in your analysis.

Review 1 Minefields

Women, surprisingly, scarcely feature in Pat Barker's latest novel. Perhaps because she is bored to tears with being described as the feminist chronicler of northern, working-class womanhood, *Regeneration* is almost entirely concerned with middle- and upper-class men.

More predictably, Barker has lighted on another excellent story: a true story, an old one, but rich in present-day literary potential ... In Barker's Craiglockhart, the wards are screaming with those who have wasted their sanity, but the core of her novel is the dialogue that develops between Sassoon and his doctor, an elderly, doubt-prone, intelligent man called Rivers. Between them, the two try to tease out the meanings of courage, duty and masculinity, while underneath their debates a flourishing father-son relationship extends the book's exploration of manhood.

So far, so engrossing. The problem is that none of it is pushed to its imaginative limits. No matter how theoretically disturbing, in practice the book remains resolutely nice: as though, in her pity for the damaged young men, Barker has decided to return them to the safety of a wholesome and sexless *Jennings* school story, a land where the worst nightmares can be soothed by matron's protective hand. The novel is far too

compassionate and serious to dislike. It is also, I should add, very readable, with one alarming passage of odd beauty and a number of interesting semi-developed ideas.

The one that had lodged in my mind is Dr Rivers's suggestion that the trenches drove so many young men insane not because they were dangerous, but because they subjected the soldiers to a helpless *passivity*: a state, in other words, not far removed from that which, in peacetime, drives so many women to breaking point.

Harriett Gilbert, *New Statesman and Society*

Review 2 The Ghost Road

The authenticity of history is useful to writers of fiction. It can be challenged or invoked; and its scale can be adjusted to amplify or to diminish human drama, either way providing props, backdrops and special effects at comparatively little imaginative cost. The dangers are obvious: fiction is authenticated by its evidence of research-details of the real place, people, technology. Anecdotes and arcane practices impress us primarily because they are 'real'.

The First World War has been extensively treated in fiction. Some of the most influential novels of this century were written in its aftermath, several by those who had fought: *All Quiet on the Western Front*, *The Good*

Soldier Schweik, A Farewell to Arms. (Even Hemingway saw a month's action before getting blown up.) A sense of disintegration and the unimaginable characterized the contemporary artistic response. The struggle to find adequate language resulted in its renewal through being broken open or pared right down.

In the 1990s, however, there can be no such struggle when writing about the First World War, no such sense of renewal. We have enjoyed decades of retrospective consensus: known good and evil, agreed right and wrong. Yet we are seeing a strange revival of interest among novelists in the subject. This may be a matter of timing, of opportunism: the war represents both a lost world and the beginnings of the place in which we now live; ancient enough to be history and recent enough to be inherited.

When writers now turn to the First World War, they must find some way of disturbing dust that is thickly settled. Otherwise they make costume drama, something too integrated and too imaginable. The British novelist Pat Barker has chosen to write a trilogy on the war. Her concerns are not those of drama and history, but of psychology and society. Still, these three novels do not escape the dangers inherent in historical fiction, and particularly the problems which flow from the size and familiarity of their subject.

Barker's early novels, based on the world of the British working-class women of her childhood, were acclaimed for their authenticity, so much so that their author felt they were being read more as sociology than fiction. So she set out deliberately to write beyond her established and expected territory as a 'northern, regional, working-class feminist,' and produced a trilogy of novels about the lives of a group of officers who were patients in the same psychiatric hospital during the First World *War* (*Regeneration, The Eye in the Door* and, most recently, *The Ghost Road*). From a subject (working-class womanhood)

that traditionally had little voice, Barker chose one which, as she has said, 'has whole libraries devoted to it.' She has made good use of them: most of the characters, and many of the events, are historical. The setting of the first book, *Regeneration*, is Craiglockhart Hospital outside Edinburgh, where the doctors include the pioneering anthropologist and neurologist W.H.R. Rivers, and where among the patients are the poets Wilfred Owen and Siegfried Sassoon. The symbolism of these three real-life figures is elaborated upon in the trilogy by appearances from or references to a number of equally famous radicals, each of whom is an obvious motif for a particular ethical dilemma, social stance or milieu. Robert Graves, Bertrand Russell, Ottoline Morrell, Sigmund Freud, Oscar Wilde, H.G. Wells, Richard Dadd and Charles Dodgson all make appearances. This is not altogether successful. The attempt to animate these personalities is hampered by the reader's prior knowledge and preconceptions, while passing allusions to a renowned pacifist or psychotic also read, irritatingly, as shorthand for what a writer should try more originally to evoke.

It is where Barker is less self-conciously factual, less awed by her research and more confident of her fiction, that the books come to life. *Regeneration* opens with Siegfried Sassoon publicly stating his refusal, in 1917, to take any further part in the war and condemning the futility of the continuing slaughter. He is diagnosed as shellshocked and consigned to Craiglockhart to be 'cured.' Rivers embarks on a gentle and gentlemanly analysis, even arranging for Sassoon to go to his Club. At the same time, Rivers also begins treatment of the belligerent Billy Prior, a working-class officer or 'temporary gentleman', who is intelligent and articulate, aspiring to amorality but with a weakness for big ideas. He proves a perturbing patient for Rivers, whom he mimics, teases and confronts, making for far more interesting reading than the mutually admiring and self-consciously understated exchanges of Rivers and Sassoon. The contrast between the two characters is instructive: it is as if Barker knew how Sassoon should speak but can let Prior find out for himself.

The First World War has been saturated in popular imagery; in addition to its literature, there is the more pervasive influence of the war movie. Alas, aspects of *Regeneration* bring these common influences to mind. As Sassoon agonizes over his position with the languid elegance of a cinematic hero and Robert Graves rushes to help with the bluff efficiency and dogged devotion of the hero's best friend, the dialogue seems disturbingly secondhand, as if, while written in one medium, it has been sieved through another – the book of the film of the war. Barker's dialogue becomes more convincing, but her narrative often takes the form of indirect speech that wobbles uncomfortably between the characters' language and Barker's own, with sudden shifts from the colloquial to the literary within the same voice. Plain language is embellished with rich metaphor, adding unlikely formal contrivances to otherwise carefully un-self-conscious speech ...

Still, there is a sense of deep engagement between Barker and her subject. Her exploration of mental and physical devastation shows us how estrangement and incapacity not only call into question identity, values and belief, but provoke the redefinition of morals, gender and sexuality. Throughout the trilogy, Prior and Rivers encompass this sense of disintegration, as they become more complex and ambiguous, and lead more dislocated lives. That Barker has chosen to write three books on the war suggests how much there is she wants to say. Perhaps as a consequence, Prior and Rivers are pushed to encompass her themes, and at times their characters are engulfed by the issues Barker so palpably wants to air ...

Lavinia Greenlaw, *The New Republic*, Washington April 29, 1996

Review 3 Among damaged men

... Its time is World War 1; its location is mainly Scotland; its characters are nearly all men – British Army officers, some of them historical figures; and its central subject is the classic male theme of war and manhood. To cross gender, class, geographical and historical lines all at once strikes me as a courageous and chancy thing for any writer to do. And to write fiction about real people who have left their own accounts of their lives is surely to gamble against the odds...

Her version begins with Sassoon's letter of resignation and ends with Rivers' last annotation in his patient's file: '*Nov. 26, 1917. Discharged to duty.*' Within these historical brackets a number of stories are told, some historical, some not. One tells how the army's Medical Corps dealt with a new problem in military medicine that it was unprepared either to understand or treat – the large number of officers and men who broke down under fire ...

These damaged men fill the hospital. To regenerate them, Rivers must help them to confront the inhumanity of the war they have experienced, and to find ways of being human within it. For Rivers, the clearest way to humanity is through *fathering*. 'Fathering,' he thinks, 'like mothering, takes many forms beyond the biological. Rivers had often been touched by the way in which young men, some of them not yet 20, spoke about feeling like fathers to their men.' If you are a father to your men, then your place is with them, whatever you may think about war.

Regeneration is historically accurate on this point: young officers from Craiglockhart who returned to the trenches did think about their fathering roles there. 'I am only here *to look after* some men,' Sassoon wrote in his diary in France in 1918; and Owen said much the same thing in a letter: 'I came out in order to help these boys.' To be a father is to be a man: but not as the army understands manhood ...

This novel, like her others, is testimony to the persistent vitality of that kind of writing. Fashions change, theories emerge and fade, but the realistic writer goes on believing that plain writing, energized by the named things of the world, can make imagined places actual and open other lives to the responsive reader, and that by living those lives through words a reader might be changed. Pat Barker must believe that, or she wouldn't write as she does. I believe it, too.

Samuel Hynes, *The New York Times*, March 29, 1992

Review 4 Soldiers of Misfortune

...It is a tribute to Barker's imaginative reach and the generosity of her feminism that she can produce such an affecting novel about the impact of war on men, and that she can so so without forfeiting the caliber of insight that distinguished *Union Street, Blow Your House Down,* and *The Century's Daughter*...

By stationing the action away from the trenches, Barker can press beyond the point where most war novels are content to end. *Regeneration* asks not just 'How does war feel?' but 'What ideals of manhood make the conduct of war possible?' and 'Why have these ideals failed?' Barker's protagonist, Dr. William Rivers, an army psychologist, inhabits the cusp between military and civilian life. This pioneering psychologist, neurologist, and anthropologist is ideally placed to grapple with the enormous issues the novel raises, most notably the crippling effects of emotional repression as a measure of manliness ...

All of Barker's work reveals her singular gift for immersing readers in the atmospherics and pathologies of violence – whether rape, murder, trench warfare, torture, or unremitting confinement. Among the victims, she reserves her greatest sympathy for young people – 19-year-old officers, 12-year-old rape survivors, 16-year-old prostitutes – whose early exposure to brutality plunges them into premature, bewildered versions of adulthood. Impatient with the official heroisms that crowd the bookshelves, Barker reiterates in *Regeneration* her attraction to the spectacular yet hidden braveries that sustain 'unliterary' lives. (She's more impressed by Sassoon's inconspicuous than his public gallantry. His most impressive act of bravery, she suggests, is to deny his own need to be *seen* as hyper-masculine.) Few novelists are so unsentimentally animated by people's ability to chalk up small, shaky, but estimable victories over remorseless circumstances. Readers come away from all her novels with an altered feeling for the boundaries and capacities of human courage.

Rob Nixon, *Voice*, July 14 1992

The film of *Regeneration*

A close reading of one key episode – Prior's recovery of his memories of the Front (1:07:54)

- Re-read Chapter 9, from the bottom of page 98 to the end of the chapter.

- Talk about what key aspects of the novel are being explored at this point, in terms of:
  - characters
  - oppositions and issues
  - language
  - plot development.

- Think about how easy or difficult it would be to adapt as a film. Make a list of the problems and possibilities. Talk about how you would tackle it if you were the film director.

- Now look at the film clip on the video. Watch it once and talk about first responses.

- Now watch it a second time. This time, share out responsibility for looking closely at the different aspects of the filming listed below.

  - The camera – what's interesting about camera angles, the point of view from which shots are taken, what's in focus and out of focus, how shots are framed, who's in the frame and their relative size and position in relation to each other.
  - The sound – how music, sound effects and silence are used and what key ideas are reinforced by the use of sound.
  - The use of the flashback – how the shift to the flashback and back again takes place, what's different about the visual style of the flashback compared with the rest of the film.
  - Mise en scène – the visual style and design of Rivers' office and the flashback scenes.
  - The acting – how the relationship between Rivers and Prior is conveyed, how changes in the two characters are marked and how the drama of this key moment in their relationship is created.
  - The way in which the director uses the metaphor of the eye. Think, not only in terms of the literal 'gobstopper' eye but also other ways in which the idea of the eye is used, such as the way characters look, or are looked at by others. (The next book in the trilogy is called *The Eye in the Door*.)

- Share your observations and add anything else that struck you as interesting.

What is this director's interpretation?

Gillies McKinnon's adaptation of this episode is an 'interpretation' of it. He has chosen to foreground some things, play down some things and completely ignore others.

- Talk about what he has chosen to do with key aspects of the novel, such as:
  - how the characters are represented
  - which oppositions or issues are foregrounded in the scenes in the film
  - how ideas and thoughts, that are made explicit through third person narration in the book, are conveyed filmically.

- Talk about which aspects of the interpretation:
  - you agree with strongly
  - you disagree with strongly
  - you find particularly interesting or successful
  - you find puzzling or unsatisfactory
  - have given you fresh insights into the book.

- You could write a close comparison between this episode of the book and the film adaptation as an essay for internal assessment, or as preparation for synoptic work on texts about the First World War.

A good adaptation? A good film?

In her video interview, Pat Barker praised the Director of the film. However, she also said, 'I don't think film is an appropriate medium really for exploring ideas.'

- Having looked closely at the adaptation of Chapter 9, do you agree with her view?

- Watch the video interview of Barker talking about the film. If you have the opportunity to watch the whole film, talk about:
  - how successfully you think it works as an adaptation
  - how well it explores the ideas of the book
  - to what extent it is an 'interpretation' of the book and what the interesting features of this interpretation are
  - what is gained or lost by the elements of the book that are missing (such as the Aldeburgh scenes with Burns, the relationship with Henry and Ruth Head and so on).

Reviews of the film

- Read the reviews of the film on pages 121 and 122 . Annotate them to identify ideas you agree with, disagree with or find particularly interesting or helpful.

- Write your own review of the film, drawing on what you know of the book, the author's views and the views of other reviewers, to discuss how successful you find it both as an adaptation and as a film in its own right.

Review 1 Welcome to the killing zone

The first image of Gillies MacKinnon's *Regeneration* (18) is a shocking aerial view of the First World War trenches: acres of devastated land, men and corpses riddling the mud like fossil seashells. Its scale is so extraordinary that when MacKinnon makes a bathetic shift into standard Brit-Lit cinema, his film becomes a casualty of its opening shot. Adapted from Pat Barker's novel, the film focuses on Craiglockhart Military Hospital, where inmates Wilfred Owen (Stuart Bunce) and Siegfried Sassoon (James Wilby) are undergoing treatment by psychiatrist WHR Rivers (Jonathan Pryce). While the poets flirt and recite future A-level texts to each other, Rivers becomes slowly unnerved by his patients' accounts of the slaughter in France. Though his pioneering techniques facilitate the regeneration of the title, we learn frustratingly little about them. We see the gruesome alternatives – in the form of John Neville's electrode-happy Dr Yealland – but Rivers's experimentally non-punitive psychoanalytic methods go unexplained – presumably because Freud is less fashionable than decorous costume drama. But despite the attention to period veracity, the purely fictional part of the story is where the film rings most true, principally in the story of shellshocked Billy Prior (*Trainspotting*'s Jonny Lee Miller, blazingly good as another sick boy) and Sarah Lumb, the young nurse who befriends him (a razor-sharp Tanya Allen).

The Independent, November 23 1997

Review 2 Rhetoric Rather than Reality

(In this film) war is an odd, distant thing, like the wail of a cosmic tinnitus. *Regeneration* opens with a stupendous overhead shot across a battlefield, whose corpse-strewn wastes and smoking trenches are like Stanley Spencer out of Hieronymus Bosch.

The intensity is sustained in the first scene at Craiglockhart Castle, the army's mental curatorium. We watch Sassoon's fellow poet Wilfred Owen (Stuart Bunce) wander a wintry, crow-cawing wood, like a man painting the iconography of his mind even as he walks through it.

But then the talk starts – and never really stops. As James Wilby's flimsily drawn Sassoon locks mind with Jonathan Pryce's tormented but liberal-minded psychiatrist Rivers, *Regeneration* begins to ache with loaded argument and moral complacence. Pryce/Rivers's humane treatment methods are scripted to form a buddyish bond with Sassoon's poetic pacifism, while we are encouraged to hiss and boo at the facile walk-on demons: from the military establishment to the batty aversion therapist (John Neville) who treats shellshock with physical pain.

Gone are the complicating mid-tones of Barker's novel: its homo-eroticism (we would barely know Sassoon was gay) or its delving in the minutiae of Rivers's methods. And gone is any *raison d'etre* for the fourth main character, the Everyman-ish young tommy (Jonny Lee Miller) who gained pointfulness on the page by echoing on into the remainder of Barker's trilogy. His function here is simply to stand about megaphoning the obvious. 'Maybe you're the one who's ill,' he tells Pryce, in one of the film's all too typical bursts of R.D. Laing for simpletons.

Nigel Andrews, *The Financial Times*, November 20 1997

Review 3 Poetry, soldiers and war

Through the use of flashbacks, the film vividly captures the horrors of trench warfare. Many of the scenes are uncompromising in their depiction of the brutality and tragic waste. The connection between the experience of the trenches and the state of mind of the soldier-patients at Craiglockhart is developed through a series of dream-like images.

The film depicts the increasing tensions and uncertainties that were developing in the army. The orchestrated calm of the hospital breakfast table is regularly disrupted by news from the front. At one point Sassoon reads out the casualty figures from the morning newspaper, and points out the name of a young soldier he knew. There is a bewildered and uncomfortable silence around the table. Sassoon is enraged at what he perceives as a general lack of sympathy. Rivers, in turn, is angered at Sassoon for disrupting his patients 'recovery'.

Rivers is far more attuned to the sensibilities of the ordinary army soldier than most of those in his profession. While on forced leave, due to exhaustion, he travels to London to visit an old friend and fellow neurologist. Dr Yealland. Like Rivers, Yealland is now involved in treating those psychologically damaged by the war, but he employs rather different methods. Rivers is sickened when his friend straps a patient suffering from mutism into a chair and electrically tortures him into speaking. Yealland boasts afterwards that his department has a 100% success rate. Rivers begins

to question the morality of a process whereby he certifies men as sane only to send them back to the very situation that initially robbed them of their sanity.

Gillies Mackinnon (who also directed *Small Faces*) does an admirable job in bringing a fascinating story to the screen. There are a number of impressive performances, particularly those of Pryce and Miller. One of the strengths of the original story is the power of the dialogue between the main characters. This is faithfully conveyed in the film.

Regeneration was poorly promoted and only played at selected cinemas. It would be an unjust fate for this well-acted and brilliantly shot film to remain relatively unknown. I hope its video release will enable it to reach the wider audience it deserves. It should also encourage a reading of Pat Barker's trilogy, which provides a compelling study of real-life figures, as well as fictitious characters, to illustrate the human tragedy of the war.

Harvey Thompson, *World Socialist Web Site*

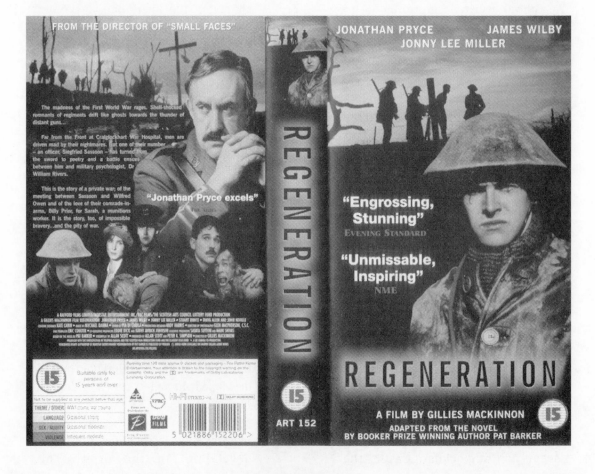

A scene by scene synopsis of the film

Using the synopsis

This scene by scene synopsis of the film can be used to help you compare the film adaptation with the novel. Use it in conjunction with the chapter summaries on page 125-126, to look at shifts in sequencing, changes of setting and the process of selection and foregrounding that took place in adapting the book for the screen.

1. The desolation of the trenches – filmed from above in near-monotone.

2. Owen finds Burns, naked, in the circle of dead animals.

3. Craiglockhart Hospital – key characters are introduced. Prior walks up towards the building.

4. Owen brings Burns back and hands him over to Rivers.

5. Prior's nightmares in the night.

6. Scene from the front – Sassoon (not yet introduced as such), checking men's feet, the death of his friend, Sassoon's heroic storming of a German position.

7. Sassoon throws away his medal.

8. Sassoon's declaration intercut with his arrival at Craiglockhart.

9. Rivers, after talking to Bryce, decides to take Sassoon on as a patient.

10. Rivers and Sassoon talk in the corridor and continue in first therapeutic conversation. Scene ends with Rivers reassuring Campbell that Sassoon isn't a spy.

11. Prior and Rivers' first 'conversation', with Prior mute and writing notes.

12. Campbell tells Rivers he thinks Sassoon is a German spy.

13. Rivers in his bedroom, reading the poems given to him by Sassoon.

14. Arrival of Graves.

15. Rivers and Sassoon on steps of hospital, talking about whether Sassoon might find it difficult to be 'safe' while others die.

16. Burns vomiting at meal time.

17. Rivers and Burns, in Burns' room.

18. Graves' departure.

19. Sassoon tells Rivers that he may leave and get a Harley St. doctor to declare him sane.

20. Owen in the grounds – what seems to be a flashback to war but turns out to be a 'flashforward' to his own death.

21. War Office inspector arrives at Craiglockhart – various scenes showing his displeasure at the nature of the treatment (army of small boys, paper boats etc.).

22. Prior and Rivers – Prior's voice has returned. Flashback to young soldier tied to post at front because of breaking down.

23. War Office inspector complaining of 'loose rods' on the stair carpet.

24. Sassoon playing golf in grounds – approached by Owen for autograph. Talks of the skulls being as ancient as from Marlborough's army.

25. Rivers returns to Craiglockhart in his car in the dark. Stops and sees Prior. Starts to stammer.

26. The doctors discuss Prior and Sassoon's cases with Rivers.

27. Rivers and Sassoon talk on a pier by the sea – Sassoon on a bicycle, Rivers in his car.

28. Prior and Rivers in the consulting room. Flashback to Prior's gradually returning memory of the attack when he became mute.

29. At breakfast, Sassoon confronts Rivers about the newspaper report of a 17 year old who's been killed.

30. Prior goes into town and meets Sarah.

31. Sassoon and Owen talk about poetry, in the grounds of the hospital.

32. Prior and Sarah alone in the bar.

33. Prior and Sarah walk in the cloisters – sexual tension between them.

34. Prior and Rivers argue about Prior's confinement to the hospital and Prior says 'Maybe you're the one who's ill.'

35. Owen and Sassoon work on the poems – flashforward to the scene of Owen's death, without the audience being aware of it being this and flashback to Burns, naked.

36. Prior comes to say sorry to Rivers. Rivers decides to hypnotise him there and then – flashback to his forgotten memories of the events with the eye, 'a gobstopper'.

37. Prior and Rivers continue to talk in the grounds.

38. Owen leaves his poems for Sassoon.

39. Rivers and Sassoon discuss the forthcoming Medical Board.

40. Sarah and Madge visit Madge's sweetheart in the hospital.

41. Owen and Sassoon work on 'Anthem for Doomed Youth'.

42. Sarah and Prior talk in the bar, after Billy's confinement to the hospital.

43. Prior and Sarah make love at the seaside – a flashback to the battle field.

44. The patients play catch with a hat in the hall – Rivers joins in but is clearly ill and falls on the stairs.

45. Rivers treats Willard, who is convinced he's paralysed. Rivers is shown to be on the verge of nervous collapse.

46. Rivers is examined by Bryce – feeling 'shellshocked' by his

patients. They talk about Henry Head and the experiments on the regeneration of nerves.

47. Rivers' departure for London.

48. Rivers' goes to see Yealland's treatment. Witnesses the treatment of Callan.

49. Rivers is back at Craiglockhart. Talks to Sassoon about Yealland's treatment. Sassoon gives him moral support.

50. Rivers talks to Prior about his asthma and the forthcoming Medical Board. Prior wants to return, to be part of 'the club to end all clubs'.

51. Prior, Sassoon and others wait for the Medical Board. Sassoon leaves in disgust and packs his bags.

52. Prior attends the Medical Board.

53. Rivers searches for Sassoon, checks his room and finds him gone.

54. Rivers finds Sassoon with Owen, in the grounds. A passionate argument ends in a sense of how much he means to Sassoon.

55. Burns, who is leaving Craiglockhart, says goodbye to Rivers.

56. Bryce and Rivers talk about Burns.

57. Prior is upset at being given Home Service. Shakes Rivers' hand and asks if he can write to him.

58. Rivers in his bed at night – obviously troubled.

59. Sassoon's hallucination of dead men, crowding round his bed.

60. Sassoon tell Rivers about the hallucinations and the fact that he's decided to go back to the Front.

61. Sassoon's Medical Board.

62. Discussion by the Board of Sassoon's case.

63. Rivers talks to Sassoon after the Board. Sassoon makes it clear he thinks Rivers has also been 'wounded' by his experience of the war.

64. Bryce and Rivers talk – Rivers expresses doubts about whether he's done the right thing with Sassoon.

65. Owen and Sassoon's farewell.

66. A long sequence of shots, without dialogue, showing: Sassoon's departure in the rain; Rivers walking in the grounds with other patients; Prior and Sarah in bed together; Owen leaving in a bus; troops at the front squelching through mud; Sassoon at the front – injured in the head and laughing; German soldiers surrendering; bells ringing at Craiglockhart for the end of the war; the canal tunnel that occurred previously in scenes with Owen, which now zooms in on his dead body. (It finally becomes clear that this is the scene of his death.)

67. Rivers receives a letter from Sassoon telling of Owen's death.

68. As Rivers reads, he hears the voice of Owen telling the story of Abraham and Isaac. The film ends with Rivers weeping.

Chapter summary

Part 1

1. Sassoon's 'A Soldier's Declaration'. Bryce and Rivers discuss his case and Rivers accepts him as a patient. Sassoon's memory of a conversation with Robert Graves about whether he'll be court martialled. His arrival at Craiglockhart.

2. Sassoon and Rivers' first consultation – Sassoon's motivations are explored. Burns' vomiting – the story of Burns' experience – landing in the man's intestines, mouth filled with rotting body.

3. Graves' arrival – tells Rivers how he lied to Sassoon about never being court-martialled. Rivers reads Sassoon's poems – idea of poems as a form of therapy.

4. Anderson's dreams – Rivers' interpretations. Sassoon and Rivers – first suggestion of Rivers as father-figure for Sassoon. Story of Sassoon's father leaving, then dying – the army is *probably the only place I've ever really belonged.'* Burns' flight – dead animals on the tree.

5. Introduction of Prior – unable to speak, uncooperative. Sassoon sees Graves off in Edinburgh. Rivers' dream about his friend Henry Head – way of introducing the experiment on the regeneration of nerves that they'd conducted on Head. Conflict in Rivers – between desire to give treatment and sense that the pain involved was sometimes too great. Rivers' feeling that, in encouraging the men to uncover repressed feelings, he's setting himself up against everything they've ever been taught to do. Becomes aware of the implications for himself. He was a product of the same system.

6. Return of Prior's voice – aggressive attitude towards Rivers. They discuss hypnosis. Sassoon's contacts with pacifists & others – Bertrand Russell, Edward Carpenter, Robert Ross. Allusions to Sassoon's sexuality. Prior's father and mother come to Craiglockhart – issues to do with class and aspirations – Billy's asthma is revealed. Broadbent – thinks he's a captain – says he needs to visit his sick mother. Prior's wheezing – asthma attack.

7. Prior and Rivers – discuss transference, father figures – Prior's clever cynicism. Talk about class/snobbery in the army. Rivers and Sassoon talk over breakfast, after reading the newspaper – Sassoon's letter & Platt's death at 17 – Rivers starts to stammer. Rivers' medical notes on Sassoon – discussion with other doctors, Bryce and Brock. Discussion with Brock – raises idea of Sassoon being in a 'protopathic' phase. Also idea of Rivers' own mental state needing consideration.

Part 2

8. Prior's attempts to recover the memories of what happened – that the attack felt 'sexy.' Owen and Sassoon meet for the first time. Owen on the war – as if the trenches are 'ancient'. Prior meets Sarah Lumb in the café. Sarah and her mother – different views on men. Sarah and Prior in the churchyard.

9. Prior and Rivers – Prior in trouble for not wearing his badge. Talk about mutism, stammering and class – officers don't suffer from it. Stammering more common in officers. Physical illnesses in private soldiers. Prior turns focus on Rivers' stammer. Question of whether Rivers is in need of treatment himself. Men scything without their shirts – Rivers' regret that they're forced to put them on again. Prior apologises to Rivers – talks to him about his nightmares being muddled up with sex. Rivers decides to try hypnosis now. Prior's memories of the eye – Prior had thought the death of the men must have been his fault. Rivers' view that breakdown isn't a reaction to a single event – it's more like 'erosion'. Prior's difficulty in accepting he could break down. Rivers himself not feeling well. Nanny goat image. Young men feeling like fathers to the soldiers under their command. Idea that in this war, stagnating in holes denied them 'manly activity' and delivered 'feminine' passivity – this seen as a cause for breakdown.

10. Talk between Lizzie, Sarah, Madge and other women. For Lizzie, when war was declared, *'Peace broke out.'* Says she'll get herself some false teeth and have a *'bloody good time'*. Rivers' treatment of Willard, who can't walk. Sassoon meets Rivers at the Conservative Club. Sassoon makes it impossible for Rivers to suppress his knowledge that it is the war that is making men break down.

11. Owen and Sassoon talk about Rivers and Owen's poem.

12. Sarah and Prior by the sea. His feelings about class are explored – he feels at home with her.

13. Rivers' recommendation that Burns should be given an unconditional discharge. Prior has another asthma attack in the train on the way home. Discussion with Rivers of whether the asthma might prevent him from going back to the front. Rivers' belief that the war will change the class system. Anderson's panic attack after seeing blood. Rivers' strain showing – complains of *'feeling quite ill.'* Pain in his chest. Believes it to be 'war neurosis'. Goes on leave. Sassoon and Owen draft 'Anthem for Doomed Youth'. Sassoon believes that a member of his platoon, Orme, is in his room, by the door. Discovers Rivers has gone on leave. Sense of loss. Memories of himself aged 5, the day his father left home.

Part 3

14. Rivers in church. Listens to the Biblical story of Abraham's sacrifice of Isaac. Thinks of its relevance to the war – the young men betrayed by their elders. Stays at the chicken farm with his brother Charles and his wife, Bertha. Memories of his childhood – Reverend Charles Dodgson (Lewis Carroll), who disliked boys; his father, who treated stammerers; his challenge to his father over Darwin. Link with Sassoon. Drafting of 'Anthem for Doomed Youth.' Madge and Sarah visit Madge's sweetheart in the hospital. Sarah blunders into the ward with the men in wheelchairs. Prior is examined by a medical doctor at the hospital, to see if he's fit. Sees Sarah. Rivers' walk with Ruth Head who supports Sassoon's stand. Head offers Rivers a job in London, with the Royal Flying Corps.

15. Burns' home in Aldeburgh. Reference to the paper Rivers was writing about patients suppressing their memories of war experience. Burns hides in the moat – Rivers' reflection that nothing justifies suffering. Burns begins to talk about the war managing to 'put the decomposing corpse into some kind of perspective.' Rivers' sense of horror increases at the realisation of the 'complete disintegration of personality' produced by the experience of war.

16. Rivers' return to Craiglockhart. Begins to see that he could connect his work in anthropology with his work with patients. Recognition of the importance of his work with his patients. Sassoon tells Rivers about his hallucination – Orme coming to his room. Rivers tells him about his supernatural experience in the Solomon Islands – spirits coming to carry the dead person's soul away. Sassoon's poem about the need to go back. Rivers and Sassoon – parent/child relationship.

Part 4

17. Ada Lumb comes to see Sarah. Her view of men, as compared with Sarah's, is presented. Argument between Graves and Sassoon about 'keeping your word' by staying with the men, even if your views about the rights and wrongs of the war have changed – it's like a contract. Discussion about sexuality – Graves suggests that he's no longer interested in men – has met a woman. A boy he knew at school is arrested for soliciting and being sent to Rivers to be 'cured.' Sassoon tells Rivers.

18. The Medical Board – Prior's conflicting feelings about getting permanent home service. Prior's suggestion that Rivers isn't so much like a father-figure as a mother-figure to him – mention of the nanny goat. Sassoon doesn't wait for the Board. Conversation with Rivers – head boy/headmaster analogy. Sassoon is thinking of continuing the protest – decides that he wants to go back.

19. Prior and Sarah in her room. 'He needed her ignorance to hide in. Yet, at the same time, he wanted to know and be known as deeply as possible. And the two desires were irreconcilable.' Owen and Sassoon say good-bye to each other. News that Rivers is going to leave Craiglockhart.

20. Rivers and Sassoon talk. Rivers is worried that Sassoon has given up hope. Rivers' departure for London. Interest in the differences between breakdown across the different branches of the airforce – Rivers' view that it is the passivity of war which does the most damage. Connection is made with the breakdown of women in peacetime. Visit to Yealland's hospital: 'in every case the removal of the physical symptom was described as a cure.' Sees Callan, the patient who can't speak and requests that he should see his treatment. The electric shock treatment of Callan by Yealland.

21. Rivers' illness – the 'confrontation' with Yealland is troubling him. He has feverish dreams, involving: Yealland; Sassoon's protest; a man with a horse's bit in his mouth. The dream seems to be saying that he's no different to Yealland. Yealland, in making Callan speak, was actually silencing his protest. Rivers feels, in his own way, he's doing the same. Decides the dream is about Sassoon and the silencing of his protest – his influence on him and his feelings of guilt about Sassoon going back.

22. Rivers' discussion with Henry Head about his feelings. Tells Head about his life-changing experience in the Solomon islands. Feels that the patients have changed him – they've done for him what he couldn't do for himself. Rivers' return to Craiglockhart. Anderson is still a mess. Sassoon has a fresh medical board. Rivers speaks in favour of him being sent back into service. Sassoon refuses to recant but is clear about wanting to go back. Rivers' feelings are explored – his doubts, his changed attitudes, his concerns for Sassoon and the influence of Sassoon on him.

Teachers' notes

A route through the novel

● 'Exploring the contexts of the novel' on pages 76-84 offers contextual material and a way into reading and reflecting on the first chapter of the novel.

● Students should then read the rest of the novel. You could pause at key points, such as at the end of each of the four parts, to share views, questions and difficulties. The student material suggests using 'post-it' notes, to mark on the book questions and issues that can be explored in the class.

● Activities on the structure of the novel, narrative viewpoint and character, in the student material, could be offered either during or after reading. (For instance, the work on 'characters and oppositions' on page 87 could be started during reading and returned to after reading, to be developed more fully.)

The interview

Students might find it helpful to watch the interview with Pat Barker soon after their first reading, before going on to look more closely at key aspects of the novel.

Exploring the contexts of the novel (pages 76-84)

You could take this understanding of the contexts of the fiction further by doing the role play on First World War poetry in *Text, Reader, Critic* (EMC Advanced Literature Series).

Reading *Regeneration* from different critical positions (pages 113-114)

The readings offer a starting-point for thinking about different literary critical positions, with some 'exaggerated' readings from different stances. You could go on to explore these ideas in more detail using the Critical Position Cards from *Text, Reader, Critic*.

Using the film

There are two clips from the film on the video: the opening of the film and the hypnotising of Prior.

The opening is used as a way of exploring the context of the First World War, on page 77.
The clip about the hypnotising of Prior appears on page 119, as a more fully developed analytical activity looking at the way the book has been adapted as film. This could lead into a more extensive piece of writing, possibly for internal assessment, about the relationship between the film and the book and the film as an interpretation of the book.
A scene by scene synopsis of the film is provided, to allow close comparison of the sequencing of events, what has been omitted, how settings have been used, how static conversations in the novel are broken up so that they occur in smaller segments in different locations and so on. Used in conjunction with the 'Chapter summary' of the novel, it is a useful tool for comparing the book and the film.
The interview with Pat Barker and the film reviews provide another dimension, helping students to make evaluative judgements and think about their own readings of both the book and the film by comparison with those made by other 'readers'.